TOP **10**
SICILY

ELAINE TRIGIANI

D1021397

DK

EYEWITNESS TRAVEL

Left **Greek Theatre, Taormina** Right **Children on the beach**

LONDON, NEW YORK,
MELBOURNE, MUNICH AND DELHI
www.dk.com

Produced by Sargasso Media Ltd, London

Printed in China

First American Edition, 2003
15 16 17 18 10 9 8 7 6 5 4 3 2 1

Published in the United States by DK Publishing,
375 Hudson Street, New York, New York 10014

**Copyright 2003, 2015 © Dorling Kindersley
Limited, London**

**Reprinted with revisions 2005, 2007,
2009, 2011, 2013, 2015**

Published in the UK by Dorling Kindersley Limited
A Pengiun Random House Company

A catalog record for this book is available from the
Library of Congress

ISSN 1479-344X
ISBN 978-1-46542-924-7

Within each Top 10 list in this book, no hierarchy of
quality or popularity is implied. All 10 are, in the
editor's opinion, of roughly equal merit.

Floors are referred to throughout in accordance
with European usage; ie the "first floor" is the floor
above ground level.

MIX
Paper from
responsible sources
FSC
www.fsc.org   FSC™ C018179

Contents

Sicily's Top 10

The information in this DK Eyewitness Top 10 Travel Guide is checked regularly.
Every effort has been made to ensure that this book is as up-to-date as possible at the time of
going to press. Some details, however, such as telephone numbers, opening hours, prices,
gallery hanging arrangements and travel information are liable to change. The publishers
cannot accept responsibility for any consequences arising from the use of this book, nor for
any material on third party websites, and cannot guarantee that any website address in this
book will be a suitable source of travel information. We value the views and suggestions of
our readers very highly. Please write to: Publisher, DK Eyewitness Travel Guides,
Dorling Kindersley, 80 Strand, London, UK WC2R 0RL, or email: travelguides@dk.com.

Cover: Front – **Corbis**: Peter Barritt main; **DK Images**: John Heseltine bl. Spine – **DK Images**: John Heseltine b.
Back – **Alamy Images**: Stephen Saks Photography tr; **DK Images**: Demetrio Carrasco tc, tl.

Left **Stromboli, Aeolian Islands** Right **Salt fields, Motya**

Left **Ragusa** Right **Orecchio di Dioniso, Syracuse**

Key to abbreviations
Adm *admission charge* **Free** *no admission charge* **Dis. access** *disabled access*

3

SICILY'S TOP 10

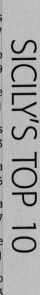

SICILY'S TOP 10

🔟 Sicily's Highlights

The island of Sicily is Italy's largest region and is also its most varied. In terms of geography, there are offshore islands, endless coastline, rugged mountains, rolling wheatfields and volcanoes, but its history and architecture are also of note. Sicily formed a significant portion of the Greek empire, was strategically vital to Rome, and was invaded in succession by the Byzantines, Arabs, Normans, French, Spanish and Bourbons, before unifying with Italy. Each conquest left its mark, to create a palimpsest of cultures on the island.

Norman Palermo 1
Norman rule of Sicily only lasted a century, but it left a rich legacy of law, culture and architecture. Their early monuments are grouped around a fortified site in the heart of Palermo *(see pp8–9)*.

Monreale 2
The last and most spectacular of the Norman monuments, the mosaic cycle at Monreale Cathedral is one of the wonders of the medieval world *(see pp10–11)*.

Aeolian Islands 3
Volcanic activity lent to each of these seven islands its own land and seascape. Evidence of 6,000 years of history, a live volcano, black lava beaches, the magnificently limpid sea, and food and wines intensely flavoured by the sun are well worth the trip out *(see pp12–13)*.

Taormina 4
As Sicily's first resort and an obligatory stop on the Grand Tour, Taormina has welcomed visitors for centuries. The town, draped with bougainvillea, offers breathtaking views, an ancient theatre, and cafés and terraces overlooking the sea *(see pp14–15)*.

Mount Etna 5
This, the largest and most active volcano in Europe, has been threatening the island since before records began. Its awesome presence dominates eastern Sicily *(see pp16–17)*.

Map locations: San Víto lo Capo, Mondello, Castellammare del Golfo, **1** Palermo, **2** Monreale, Trapani, Alcamo, Villafrati, Salemi, Gibellina Vecchia, Corleone, Castelvetrano, Chiusa Sclafar, Mazara del Vallo, **10** Selinunte, Sciacca, Ribera, Agriger, 9

Noto

Destroyed by an earthquake in 1693, Noto was rebuilt during the 1700s, when the Baroque style was at its height. A unified building programme creates harmony between landscape and village *(see pp22–3)*.

Syracuse

The once mighty Greek colony and rival to Athens quietly exists today as a thriving modern city endowed with vestiges of its former glory *(see pp18–21)*.

3 Aeolian Islands

Milazzo

Capo d'Orlando

Patti

Cefalù

San Fratello

Castelbuono

Monti

Nebrodi

Madonie

Monti

Randazzo

Taormina **4**

Caltavuturo

Nicosia

Mount Etna **5**

Vallelùnga Pratameno

Adrano

Paternò

Acireale

ofranco

Enna

Catania

Caltanissetta

Canicattì

8 Villa Romana del Casale

Palagonia

Campobello di Licata

Caltagirone

Lentini

Vizzini

Augusta

ata

Gela

Giarratana

6 Syracuse

Vittoria

Ragusa

Modica **7**

Noto

Scicli

Ispica

20 ⌐——— miles ¬0 ⌐ km ——¬ 20

Villa Romana del Casale

The extensive mosaic decorations of this luxurious Roman hunting villa are the best preserved of their kind in the world *(see pp24–5)*.

Agrigento

The famed Valle dei Templi is home to ruined Greek temples that stand, or partially stand, against a backdrop of the distant sea. They are as awe-inspiring today as they must have been to the peoples who constructed them 2,500 years ago *(see pp26–9)*.

Selinunte

Another of Sicily's remarkable ancient sites, the romantic remains of Greek Selinus reign spectacularly from a promontory high above the sea. Comprising the largest archaeological park in Europe, Selinunte offers the chance for a solitary ramble among the ruins, walking in the footsteps of history *(see pp30–33)*.

🔟 Norman Palermo

When the Normans entered Palermo in 1071, Count Roger (see p36) favoured living in the Arab fortified palace on the highest point of the city, rather than the former seat of government in La Kalsa (see p82). The building was refortified and renamed the Palazzo dei Normanni (Norman Palace). Along with the construction of the church of San Giovanni degli Eremiti and the cathedral, Palermo soon came to represent the Norman architectural and decorative ideal. After centuries of renovations, the cathedral has become uniquely Sicilian in its mix of styles. The Palazzo dei Normanni has also been renovated by successive invaders, but the well-preserved private chapel, where western and Islamic elements are combined, is a jewel.

South porch, Cathedral

• Cathedral: Corso Vittorio Emanuele; Map K5; Open 7am–7pm daily; Interior: free; Crypt, Treasury and Royal Tombs: Adm €3.00
• Palazzo dei Normanni: Piazza Indipendenza; Map J6; Open 8:15am–5pm Mon, Fri, Sat (royal apartments closed Tue–Thu when parliament is in session); 8:15am–12:15pm Sun & public hols; Adm €8.50 Fri–Mon & hols, €7 Tue–Thu
• Cappella Palatina: Map J6; Open 8:15am–5pm Mon–Sat, 8:15am–noon Sun & hols; Adm €8.50 Fri–Mon & hols, €7 Tue–Thu

Top 10 Sights

1. Cappella Palatina
2. San Cataldo
3. Martorana
4. Sala di Re Ruggero
5. Cathedral Exterior
6. Cathedral Interior, Norman Tombs
7. Cathedral Treasury and Crypt
8. La Zisa
9. San Giovanni degli Eremiti
10. La Cuba

Cappella Palatina

Commissioned by Roger II in 1129, the chapel harmoniously combines western and Arab styles. The Arab ceiling is painted with animals and greenery *(below)*, and a Christ Pantocrator, by Greek masters using gold and silver *tesserae*, offers his blessing from the cupola and the apse *(centre)*.

San Cataldo

This church is a notable example of the Arabian–Norman architecture that flourished in Sicily under Norman control. Its roof has three typical red domes, as well as Arab-style parapets.

Martorana

The church of Santa Maria dell'Ammiraglio is known as Martorana for the 12th-century nun Eloisa Martorana, who used to decorate the church with marzipan fruit *(see p75)*.

Note: *Opening times and entry fees for monuments and museums throughout Sicily are subject to frequent changes.*

Sala di Re Ruggero

Decorated in 1140, this room in the Palazzo dei Normanni is a fine example of secular mosaic decoration *(above)*.

Cathedral Exterior

The cathedral was founded by the Archbishop of Palermo in 1185, on the site of a former mosque. Remains of the Norman structure include the exterior of the triple apse and the clock tower.

Cathedral Interior, Norman Tombs

Drastically altered in the 1700s, all that remains of the Norman interior are its tombs.

Cathedral Treasury and Crypt

The treasury highlight is the crown of Constance of Aragón, encrusted with gemstones and pearls *(below)* crafted in the 12th century. The crypt houses Greek and Roman sarcophagi.

La Zisa

This castle, built in the 12th century by Arab masons, is inspired by Moorish architecture. The name derives from the Arabian *al-Azīz*, meaning "splendid".

San Giovanni degli Eremiti

Founded in 1132, and set amid lush gardens, San Giovanni was the richest monastery in Sicily. Today the interior of the church has only remnants of its original decoration. Five red domes, typical of Arab masons, define the exterior. The cloister, built 50 years later, is more western in appearance.

Map of Norman Palermo

La Cuba

Constructed in 1180 for William II of Sicily as his personal recreation pavilion, La Cuba *(below)* was designed and decorated by Arab artists still living in Palermo after the Norman conquest.

The Normans in Sicily

In 1061 the Norman soldier Roger de Hautville took advantage of internal Arab conflict and invaded Sicily with a small number of crusaders. Roger was the first of five Norman kings who, over the following century, succeeded in turning Sicily into a well-run and wealthy monarchy. At the end of their reign, in 1266, they left an island endowed with splendid buildings and an exotic culture that armoniously blended Arab and western influences.

TOP10 Monreale

The cathedral at Monreale reigns high above the fertile Conca d'Oro (Golden Valley) overlooking Palermo. King William II founded the majestic cathedral and Benedictine monastery in 1174, and a medieval village soon grew up around them. Don't be fooled by the rather austere exterior – inside the cathedral is one of the wonders of the medieval world. Its spectacular decoration constitutes the most extensive and important mosaic cycle of its kind. The cathedral faces the lively Piazza Guglielmo, with palm trees and cafés, but the entrance is around to the left in Piazza Vittorio Emanuele, with a fountain in the centre.

Monreale Cathedral from Piazza Guglielmo

🔵 Have a coffee or *gelato* at the Bar Baby O' in Piazza Guglielmo.

🟢 The church is popular for weddings – if one is in progress when you visit, go to the cloisters and gardens first and return to the church after the service.

- Piazza Vittorio Emanuele
- Map C2
- 091 640 24 24
- Open 8:30am–12:45pm, 2:30–5:30pm Mon–Sat, 8–10am, 2:30–5:30pm Sun & hols
- Adm €2.50 to south transept, €2.00 to roof
- Cloister: Piazza Guglielmo; 091 640 44 03; Open 9am–1:30pm, 2–6pm Tue–Sat; 9am–1pm Mon, Sun & hols; Adm €6.00
- AST buses: from Palermo (Piazza Indipendenza) to Monreale

Top 10 Sights

1. Façade
2. Apse Exterior
3. Interior
4. Ceilings
5. Apse Mosaic of Christ
6. Apse Mosaics of Martyr Saints
7. Side Apse Mosaics
8. Cloister
9. Nave Mosaics
10. Castellaccio

Façade
The façade *(above)*, with a bronze door, is bracketed by two asymmetrical square towers and bears decorative stonework. The porch is an 18th-century addition.

Apse Exterior
In contrast to the rest of the exterior, which is relatively plain, the triple apse *(right)* is decorated with intricate stonework that forms interlacing arches of limestone and lava. See it from via del Arcivescovado, a short walk around the back of the building.

Interior
The interior is not greatly articulated but works as a support for around 6,500 sq m (70,000 sq ft) of brilliant mosaic. The granite columns bear Roman Corinthian capitals.

➡️ *An added bonus of a visit to Monreale are the stunning views of the valley, extending out to Palermo and the sea in the distance.*

Ceilings

The choir ceiling shows traces of Arab influences. The nave ceiling was restored after a fire in 1811.

Apse Mosaic of Christ

The enormous image of the Christ Pantocrator (below) embraces his followers with curved arms and outstretched hands.

Cloister

The cloister (above) combines Arab-styled arches, intricately carved capitals, and a lovely 12th-century fountain.

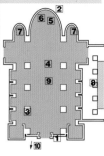

Floorplan of Monreale

Castellaccio

The 12th-century Norman castle was once a fortified monastery, but it is now used by the Sicilian Alpine Club. From its hilltop location, the castle commands a view over the valley. It is a pleasant 20-minute walk from town.

Apse Mosaics of Martyr Saints

One of the martyr saints represented is St Thomas à Becket, canonized the year before the church was founded. It is his earliest known portrait.

Nave Mosaics

These New and Old Testament scenes were educational panels for the illiterate parishioners. They include the Creation, Noah's Ark and the Sacrifice of Isaac.

Side Apse Mosaics

Above the thrones to either side of the main apse are portraits of William II being crowned by Christ himself, and presenting the cathedral to the Madonna, a scene blessed by the hand of God. The side apses (right) are dedicated to saints Peter and Paul.

King William II

According to legend, in 1174 the Madonna appeared before King William II and led him to the spot where his father had buried a considerable treasure. She instructed him to put it to good use, so William took the opportunity to create a sparkling religious monument to Sicily. Legend aside, William's political rival Walter of the Mill, Archbishop of Palermo, and his faction of landowners and clerics, had become too powerful. In building a cathedral at Monreale (specifically a Benedictine abbey and thus independent of the archbishop), William was able to redistribute the balance of power. The cathedral was finished in just under 10 years. The elaborate mosaic cycle gained fame in its own day.

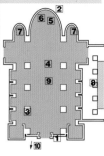

For more places of worship in Sicily See pp44–5

Aeolian Islands

With a mix of history, small-town atmosphere, intensely flavoured cuisine, and natural beauty, each of these islands has its own character. Rich in pumice, Lipari is bright white; the fertile volcanic soil of Salina grows verdant grape vines and forest; on Vulcano cooled molten lava has left entire cliffs looking like a row of elephants' legs; while on Salina rock formations rise like mounds of whipped cream. Beaches are powdery grey-white with pumice or black with powdered lava, and the sea is clean, clear and full of marine life. The islands' culture extends back 6,000 years, and there is evidence of trade with virtually every important Mediterranean culture, from the Etruscans to the Greeks.

Lipari beach

🍽 Stick to small, unassuming *trattorie* for good food at better prices.

⚠ The islands are made up of fragile volcanic stone, so watch out for falling rocks *(caduta massi)*.

• Map F1
• Aeolian Archaeological Museum: Lipari Castle; 090 988 01 74; Open 9am–1:30pm & 4–7pm (3–6pm in winter) Mon–Sat, 9am–1:30pm Sun; Adm €6.00

Top 10 Sights

1. Aeolian Archaeological Museum, Lipari
2. Marina Corta, Lipari
3. Pumice Quarries, Lipari
4. Pollara Beach, Salina
5. Perciato di Pollara, Salina
6. Sulphur Emissions, Vulcano
7. Malvasia delle Lipari
8. Stromboli
9. Panarea
10. Alicudi and Filicudi

1 Aeolian Archaeological Museum, Lipari

The museum features items from the islands' Neolithic settlements, as well as impressive Greek and Roman displays.

2 Marina Corta, Lipari

Under the castle rock, this is where the smaller craft dock *(below)*. In summer it bustles with activity; in winter you will see only the odd fisherman mending his nets.

3 Pumice Quarries, Lipari

Lipari's biggest industry used to be pumice mining, until UNESCO urged the government to stop industrial exploitation. Pumice is still so plentiful you'll find little bits of it washing up onto beaches, bobbing in the water and on sale in shops. Thanks to pumice dust on the sea-bed, the water refracts colours from turquoise to emerald.

There are ferries to the islands from Milazzo, Palermo, Naples and Messina.

Pollara Beach, Salina

The beach at Pollara *(above)* has large pebbles as well as patches of sand. The water is great for snorkelling, with sea urchins and octopuses.

Sulphur Emissions, Vulcano

Although it's a spent volcano, Vulcano still has constant sulphur emissions seeping out of the main crater, and all over the island the vapour rises out of the craggy ground. It turns the earth lurid yellows and reds and forms the *fanghi* (mudbaths) and hot bubbles in the sea.

Panarea

This is the smallest island of the archipelago and the most exclusive. Chic Panarea *(below)* is known for its coves, clear water, rocky islets and nightlife. It also has an archaeological site: a Bronze Age settlement on the Punta Milazzese.

Alicudi and Filicudi

Tiny Alicudi and Filicudi are the westernmost and least developed islands of the archipelago. Many visitors and locals call these the prettiest of the Aeolian Islands, with their natural beauty, sparse population, lack of cars and whitewashed houses with breezy terraces.

Perciato di Pollara, Salina

This stone bridge swoops down from the cliff and rests in the water, creating a natural rock bridge *(above)*. You can get to the breath-taking Perciato via land or sea and then swim around the rocks.

Malvasia delle Lipari

This is the famed product of the islands. White grapes are cultivated, harvested late and left to shrivel on cane mats before fermentation.

Stromboli

Stromboli volcano *(below)* has been active for more than two millennia, spewing sparks and red-hot rocks into the air, although you can only see them at night. Excursions are popular and available from the other islands.

Obsidian and Pumice

The two volcanic by-products obsidian and pumice have played vital roles in Lipari's commerce. The heavy, dense, glass-like black obsidian was crafted into knives and arrowheads in the Neolithic period and was highly valued and widely traded. The quarrying of white, porous pumice is the major industry at Lipari, where the enormous quarries grind the rock for use in a variety of industries worldwide.

The Aeolian Islands have been a UNESCO World Heritage Site since 2000.

🔟 Taormina

On a spectacular site on Monte Tauro, with views of the rocky coastline, the blue-green sea and the breathtaking Mount Etna, Tauromenium was founded in 304 BC as a colony of powerful Syracuse. The town endured a typical Sicilian history, falling first to the Romans, then to the Arabs, Normans and Spanish. However, during the 1800s it became an obligatory stop on the Grand Tour and life changed forever – Taormina has been host to foreign visitors ever since and, unlike much of the island, is well equipped to cater to them. The plethora of hotels, restaurants and shops, as well as beaches and manicured gardens, makes it Sicily's most popular holiday destination.

View of Taormina

🔵 After visiting the Greek Theatre, stop at the Wunderbar Café (Piazza IX Aprile 7) for a drink and some people-watching.

• Map H3
• Greek Theatre Via Teatro Greco 12, 0942 23 220, Open 9am–7pm daily; Adm €8.00

Top 10 Sights

1️⃣ Greek Theatre
2️⃣ View and Acoustics
3️⃣ Corso Umberto I
4️⃣ Piazza Vittorio Emanuele
5️⃣ Piazza IX Aprile
6️⃣ Borgo Medievale
7️⃣ Piazza del Duomo
8️⃣ Villa Comunale Gardens
9️⃣ Castelmola Walk
🔟 Mazzarò

Greek Theatre 1️⃣
Carved out of the hillside, the theatre seen today *(right)* was refurbished by the Romans in the 1st century AD. They sacrificed some of the seats and part of the stage to make a circular arena to accommodate gladiator games.

View and Acoustics 2️⃣
The Greeks designed the theatre in the 3rd century BC, with the spectacular view *(above)* forming a backdrop to their plays. Praised for its acoustics, from the top you can eavesdrop on fellow visitors at stage level.

Corso Umberto I 3️⃣
The people of Taormina make their *passeggiata* (nightly stroll) here on the Corso, beginning at Porta Messina and crossing several lively piazzas towards the end at Porta Catania. Enjoy the plentiful bars, *gelaterie*, shops and crowds.

Piazza Vittorio Emanuele 4️⃣
This piazza boasts the Palazzo Corvaja, an architectural hybrid of Arab, Norman and Catalan Gothic elements (now a tourist office), and the Santa Caterina church backed by Roman ruins.

Piazza IX Aprile

5 On this lovely square *(above)* you are spoilt for choice between the sea views and people-watching at the many outdoor cafés. The Wunderbar plays live music in the evenings.

Piazza del Duomo

7 The Baroque fountain in the piazza bears a centaur, the symbol of Taormina, here atypically female. The 13th-century Chiesa Madre, dedicated to San Nicolò, has six ancient marble columns and a tree-of-life relief carving.

Map of Taormina

Castelmola Walk

9 From via Circonvallazione take the "Salita Castello" path to the summit of Monte Tauro to enjoy the views and the medieval castle ruins.

Mazzarò

10 Below Taormina are a few lovely beaches, such as Mazzarò. Tiny Isola Bella nearby *(above)* is linked to the coast by a strip of sand.

Villa Comunale Gardens

8 With views down to Giardini-Naxos *(see p100)*, these well-tended gardens *(below)* have palm and banana trees, birds of paradise, exotic plants, a monument to Taormina's sailors and many whimsical buildings.

Borgo Medievale

6 The clock tower *(above)* is the gateway to the medieval part of town. The Corso is narrower here, and while the shops are the same mix of clothing and souvenirs, the shopfronts have kept their medieval character.

Famous Visitors

Of the innumerable well-known names that have revelled in Taormina's beauty throughout its history are: Greek king, Pyrrhus (318–272 BC); Norman conqueror Count Roger *(see p36)*; German poet Johann Wolfgang Goethe (1749–1832); English novelist DH Lawrence (1885–1930); Kaiser Wilhelm of Germany (1859–1941); American playwright Tennessee Williams (1911–83); English author Roald Dahl (1916–90); and Hollywood movie stars Elizabeth Taylor and Richard Burton.

Sicily's Top 10

10 Mount Etna

Dominating the eastern side of the island, Mount Etna is Europe's largest volcano, with several vast craters and a height of 3,330 m (10,925 ft), and it remains one of the world's most active. To the Greeks, it was home to Hephaestus, god of fire, who used its flames and lava to forge Zeus's thunderbolts; to the Arabs it was known as Mongibello (Mountain of Mountains). Today, the Parco dell'Etna encompasses much of the volcano, encouraging farmers to produce wine, cheese, honey and fruit in the rich lavic soil. For visitors, it offers breathtaking views, great hiking and, in season, skiing – and you just might see an eruption of bright-red sparks and lava.

View of Mount Etna

🕐 Follow hiking and safety guidelines provided by the park service and join one of the various guided tours. Due to the unpredictable nature of the volcano, it is not advisable to go without a guide. Bring warm clothing, sturdy shoes and glasses to protect your eyes from blowing grit.

- Map G3
- Parco dell'Etna: 095 821 111, www. parcoetna.ct.it
- Circumetnea train: 095 541 250, www. circumetnea.it
- Rifugio Sapienza: 095 915 321; www. rifugiosapienza.com
- AST bus: from Catania to Rifugio Sapienza; 095 777 45 02; leaves Catania 8:15am daily, leaves Rifugio Sapienza 4:30pm daily
- Guides: north Etna (Linguaglossa) 095 647 833; south Etna (Nicolosi) 095 791 47 55; www.guidetnanord.com; www.etnaguide.com

Top 10 Sights

1. Circumetnea Train
2. Vegetation
3. Fauna
4. Southern and Western Slopes
5. Eastern and Northern Slopes
6. Summit Craters
7. Visitor Centres
8. Lava Flows
9. Valle del Bove
10. Hikes

Circumetnea Train
From Catania, this small, quirky, narrow-gauge private railway *(above)* passes Adrano (site of a Saracen bridge), Bronte (pistachio farms), Randazzo (Lake Gurrida and lava flows, a good place to break for lunch) and Linguaglossa (murals).

Vegetation
Etna is home to a variety of trees, from oak and chestnut in low areas, to pine and birch on higher slopes. Wild flowers including violets *(right)* flourish in the lavic soil.

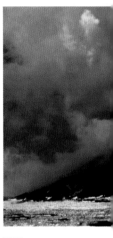

Fauna
Development has all but eliminated Etna's wolves, wild boar and deer, but small species still thrive, such as weasels and wildcats.

Southern and Western Slopes
Small volcanic cones and cultivated crops, notably pistachio farms, cover the western slopes. Recent lava flows can be seen on the south slopes.

➡ *There are also jeep excursions departing from Piano Provenzano, on the north side of the volcano.*

Eastern and Northern Slopes

On these slopes can be found the *Betula aetnensis* birch, unique to Mount Etna, and, in the town of Sant'Alfio, the *Castagno dei Cento Cavalli* (Chestnut of 100 Horses), one of the oldest and largest trees in the world. Lava flows have formed caves and grottoes, used as shelter and ice stores.

Lava Flows

Molten lava *(above)* is more than 500° C (930° F). In places, the constant flow, 2 m (6.5 ft) underfoot, causes the snow to melt.

Map of Mount Etna

Summit Craters

The summit height is constantly in flux due to mounting volcanic debris ejected during explosions and frequent landslides. The Central Crater, the Northeast Crater and the Southeast Crater emit a constant stream of sulphuric gas *(above)*.

Visitor Centre

Visitors can hook up with a trained guide at the Rifugio Sapienza Etna Sud, on the southern slope. Walks start at the top cable-car station; they vary in length and sometimes include a jeep transfer to see lava flows.

Valle del Bove

This crater *(below)* was created by partial collapse of the volcano wall. It covers 7 km by 5 km (4.5 miles by 3 miles) and has walls more than 1,000 m (3,000 ft) high. In 1991 a vent opened, releasing lava into the valley for two years.

Hikes

Hikes on lower slopes and towards the crater are possible *(above)*, safety permitting. Tourist offices provide maps and guides.

Dramatic Eruptions

In 1928, lava wiped out coastal Mascali (the only town destroyed in the 20th century), vast tracts of farmland and 550 buildings. The 1950s, 1960s and 1970s brought danger to Milo, Fornazzo, Zafferana and Sant'Alfio. A massive eruption in 1979 killed nine tourists. Between 1991 and 1993, the authorities dropped huge concrete blocks from helicopters to stop lava near Zafferana. In 1999–2002, ash covered Catania, closing the airport and roads. Lava flows in 2001 and 2002 destroyed visitors' centres and the Etna Sud cable-car station. After a respite, there were relatively modest lava flows in 2006, 2007, 2008 and 2012.

For more on Mount Etna's historic eruptions **See p104**

17

TOP 10 Syracuse

Founded in 733 BC by Corinthian settlers, Syracusae became one of the first Greek colonies on the island. It quickly attained wealth and power, commissioned important buildings and works of art, and founded sub-colonies, extending its territory through warfare to become the strongest city in the Mediterranean. The ancient city was several times the size of Syracuse today and was divided into five zones: the sparsely populated Epipolae, the necropolis zone of Akradina, residential Tyche, Neapolis (where the theatre is located), and the island of Ortygia, the original settlement.

Grotto, Latomia del Paradiso

The cafés on Ortygia come alive at sundown. Enjoy the relaxed atmosphere and cool sea breeze.

Cumulative tickets (€13.50) are available for the Archaeological Museum and park.

- Map H5
- Parco Archeologico: Viale Augusto; 0931 66 206; Open 9am–6pm daily (to 4:30pm during theatre season); Adm €10.00
- Catacombs of San Giovanni: Piazza S Giovanni; 0931 64 694; Open daily from 9:30am (closing times vary, closed for lunch); Adm €8.00
- Museo Regionale Archeologico "Paolo Orsi": Viale Teocrito 66; 0931 464 022; Open 9am–7pm Tue–Sat, 9am–1pm Sun & hols; Adm €8.00
- Castello Eurialo: 8 km (5 miles) from Syracuse; 0931 711 773; Open 9am–6:30pm summer, 9am–3:30pm winter Adm €4.00

Top 10 Sights

1. Latomia del Paradiso
2. Greek Theatre
3. Cavea
4. Temple of Apollo
5. Altar of Hieron II
6. Roman Amphitheatre
7. Catacombs of San Giovanni
8. Cathedral and Temple of Minerva
9. Museo Archeologico Regionale "Paolo Orsi"
10. Castello Eurialo

1 Latomia del Paradiso

Stone from this *latomia* (quarry) was used entirely for the construction of Syracuse. Within the quarry is the *Orecchio di Dioniso* (Ear of Dionysius) cavern *(above)*, which may have got its name from its large opening resembling a human ear.

2 Greek Theatre

Begun in the 6th century BC, the Greek Theatre *(above)* became the largest theatre in Sicily. Many of Aeschylus's tragedies were first staged here, including *Prometheus Bound*.

3 Cavea

The *cavea* (seating area) of the theatre was hewn out of rock and accommodated 15,000 spectators. Its size is still impressive today.

4 Temple of Apollo

Dating back to the 6th century BC, this is the oldest Doric temple still standing in western Europe. On the top step of the base is an inscription dedicating it to the god Apollo.

Performances of classical plays are still staged at the Greek Theatre See p62

Altar of Hieron II
Hieron II built this immense altar *(above)*, the largest in Magna Graecia, around 225 BC and dedicated it to Zeus Eleutherios, the god of freedom. Today, only the base remains.

Map of Syracuse

Castello Eurialo
The castle is the most important extant Greek military installation, built by Dionysus the Younger in the 4th century BC and later improved by Hieron II. Defensive trenches *(above)* can be accessed.

Roman Amphitheatre
The arena *(below)* was built in the 3rd century AD and is one of the largest of its kind, built by local stonemasons.

Catacombs of San Giovanni
Throughout these vast limestone catacombs are burial chambers varying in size to accommodate children, adults or families.

Cathedral and Temple of Minerva
The city's 18th-century cathedral, a sumptuous example of Sicilian Baroque religious architecture, incorporates an ancient temple of Minerva, which in turn had been built over the site of a 6th-century BC monument to Athena.

Museo Archeologico Regionale "Paolo Orsi"
Named after the archaeologist Paolo Orsi, the museum specializes in the Greek artifacts he and other scientists found during digs in Syracuse *(see pp20–21).*

Archimedes
Archimedes (287–212 BC) the renowned mathematician, engineer and inventor, was born in Syracuse and educated in Alexandria. Among his important discoveries is the Archimedes Principle, the study of a body's displacement of its weight in water. He put many of his other inventions, such as the pulley and catapult, to use in war machines and defensive mechanisms when requested to act as military advisor to Hieron II. He was killed during the Second Punic War by a Roman soldier.

During a sacrifice at the Altar of Hieron II, as many as 400 bulls would have been put to death.

Left **Villa Landolina Gardens** Right **Gargoyles from the Temple of Athena**

Archaeology Museum Highlights

1 Villa Landolina Gardens

Villa Landolina's gardens sit on a site rich in finds from an ancient Greek necropolis, parts of Hellenistic streets and later Christian catacombs.

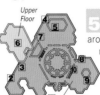

Upper Floor

Ground Floor

Museum Floorplan

2 Bronze Age Material from Castelluccio

Materials from the Castelluccio site, between Noto and Palazzolo Acreide, show trade links between early Sicilians and eastern Mediterranean cultures.

3 Material from Pantalica

Pantalica, near Palazzolo Acreide, was inhabited by the pre-Greek Sicels, who produced elegant red-glazed pottery.

4 Greek Kouros, Lentini

This 6th-century BC *kouros* (statue of a muscular youth) is one of the best examples of ancient Greek sculpture.

Bronze Age pottery

5 Mother Goddess

Made of terracotta around 500 BC, this object represents the mother goddess nursing twins. She is remarkable for the sense of solidity blended with tenderness.

6 Venus Anadyomene

A Roman copy of a Greek 2nd-century-BC original. From her pose to the high polish of the marble, she is an image of pure sensuality.

7 Temples of Athena and Apollo

Fragments from two Doric temples on Ortygia are on show, such as polychrome parts of a Gorgon.

8 Ephebus from Adrano

This small athletic bronze figure was found near Adrano, and dates from around 460 BC.

9 Gela Vase Collection

A *lekythoi* (tall one-handed vase) painted with *Herakles and the Hydra* is the most impressive.

10 Wooden Statuettes of Demeter and Kore

These rare examples of wooden statuary were found at a sanctuary between Gela and Agrigento. They date from the late 7th century BC and survived because they were covered in the mineral-rich mud of a local spring.

Discover more at www.traveldk.com

The History of Ancient Syracuse

Under the tyrant Gelon, Syracuse formed a mighty alliance with other Greeks at Akragas (Agrigento) and Gela and defeated the Carthaginians at Himera in 480 BC. Subsequent tyrants such as Hieron I (478–466 BC) and Dionysius (405–367 BC) made Syracuse the most powerful city on the island and in the Mediterranean. In 413 BC Athens sent a well-equipped fleet in what is known as the Great Expedition to put down the threat from what it saw as an upstart colony; with help from Sparta, the Athenians were sorely defeated. Despite their warlord image, Syracuse's rulers were patrons of the arts – Hieron II (265–215 BC) expanded the great theatre and Aeschylus, Pindar, Plato and Plutarch were present at court. But the end was in sight. After Hieron II's death, Syracuse sided not with Rome but with Carthage in the Second Punic Wars. After a siege lasting two years, Syracuse fell to Rome in 211 BC and began a slow decline, made final in AD 878 when the city was burned by the Arabs. Syracuse never again attained the importance it had held for centuries.

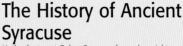

Excavating the Past

Extensive archaeological digs on the site of ancient Syracuse have been successful in uncovering remnants of that great colony such as this 5th-century BC bust *(left)* and numerous pre-Greek vases and urns *(below)*.

TOP 10 Noto

Noto is proud of its ancient origins – it was from Neas, as Noto was then known, that the Sicilian leader Ducetius led rebellions against the Greeks (see p36). After the massive earthquake that destroyed almost all of eastern Sicily in 1693, major reconstruction resulted in cities and villages being designed in the Baroque style, then at the height of popularity, and Noto is one of the best examples. Designed specifically to include vistas of the countryside, the urban plan was sensitive to the needs of the citizens and still works well today. The soft, locally quarried stone adapted well to the carved decorations, but not, unfortunately, to the elements – renovation has therefore been necessary.

Balcony, Palazzo Nicolaci

🜨 Drop into the **Caffè Sicilia**, on the Corso next to San Carlo, to sample wonderful Sicilian pastries and *gelati* made from the best local ingredients.

• Map G5
• Cattedrale di San Nicolò: Open 9am–1pm, 3–8pm daily

Top 10 Sights

1. Porta Reale
2. Chiesa di Santa Chiara & Santissimo Salvatore
3. Piazza Municipio, Palazzo Ducezio
4. Cattedrale di San Nicolò
5. San Carlo al Corso
6. Chiesa di San Domenico
7. Chiesa di Montevergini
8. Palazzi, Via Cavour
9. Old Market, Via Rocco Pirri
10. Chiesa di San Francesco

Porta Reale
The Royal Gate was erected in 1838 to greet King Ferdinand II. It offers a grand entrance to Corso Vittorio Emanuele, Noto's main street *(above)*.

Chiesa di Santa Chiara & Santissimo Salvatore
On opposite sides of the street are the convent of Santa Chiara and the monastery of Santissimo Salvatore. Santa Chiara's oval interior houses a 16th-century *Madonna and Child* sculpted by Sicilian Antonello Gagini.

Piazza Municipio, Palazzo Ducezio
The lovely town square is home to the Palazzo Ducezio, now the town hall *(below)*, designed by Sinatra in 1742. A dramatic, recessed loggia runs the length of the façade.

If you enjoy people-watching, don't miss the Sunday morning, after-church passeggiata along the Corso and Piazza Municipio.

4 Cattedrale di San Nicolò

Noto's splendid Baroque cathedral sits on top of Labisi's grand staircase. San Nicolò was built in several stages throughout the 18th century, with input from architects Gagliardi and Sinatra. Its façade is flanked by two square towers decorated with Corinthian pilasters.

6 Chiesa di San Domenico

Gagliardi's masterpiece (1737) has an exuberant, convex façade *(left and above),* which pulsates with niches and columns creating dramatic contrasts of light and shade.

7 Chiesa di Montevergini

Looking up via Nicolaci, this elegantly simple church *(below),* with its concave façade, theatrically marks the end of the street. Nearby is Palazzo Nicolaci, known for its decorated balconies supported by carved horses and grotesques.

9 Old Market, Via Rocco Pirri

Noto's lively market was at one time held in this courtyard, but sadly butchers and bakers have now been replaced by boutiques. However, there is a market in town every Monday across from San Domenico *(below).*

10 Chiesa di San Francesco

From Piazza XXX Ottobre a stairway leads to the 18th-century church of San Francesco with its noteworthy Baroque portal, stucco-decorated interior, and a wooden statue of the Virgin Mary (1564).

Baroque Architecture

The Baroque style evolved from the Renaissance, which employed Classical forms and primary shapes to create balance and proportion. Baroque architects applied these forms to curved and ovoid shapes to achieve movement and drama. Trademarks are an elliptical floorplan, a façade that projects outward or undulates, use of light and shade, concave forms, and exuberant decoration. Sicilians, in typical fashion, melded Italian Baroque with other cultures and made it their own.

5 San Carlo al Corso

Built in 1730, the church greets visitors with its graceful concave façade. The orders of the wonderfully elegant columns, with their swollen middles, progress up the façade: Doric to Ionic and finally Corinthian. The octagonal dome is silhouetted against the sky; climb up to the top for beautiful views over the town.

8 Palazzi, Via Cavour

Via Cavour is lined with *palazzi* of noble families. The Palazzo Trigona is a stately Baroque design of 1781 with characteristically curved balconies and a frescoed interior. On the corner to the left is Palazzo Battaglia, a late Baroque work by Gagliardi, and further down on the right is the Neo-Classical Palazzo Castelluccio.

Noto and seven other Baroque towns of southeastern Sicily are recognized as a UNESCO World Heritage Site.

Villa Romana del Casale

As the hunting lodge of an important Roman official (perhaps Maximianus, Diocletian's co-emperor), the villa at Piazza Armerina was decorated with what is now the best preserved and most extensive set of Roman mosaics in the world. The lavish villa was constructed over a period of more than 50 years from the late 3rd century to the early 4th century AD, and its public and private rooms, peristyles, luxurious thermal baths and gardens with pools and fountains were laid out on four natural terraces. The villa entrance was an imitation triumphal arch, while inside the house was endowed with tall ceilings and expansive rooms with open porticoes of delicate marble columns.

Garden, Villa Romana del Casale

🖰 It can get very hot inside as most of the villa is housed in a wood and plexiglass structure. Arrive early to avoid the crowds.

- Contrada Casale, 6 km (3.5 miles) from Piazza Armerina; in summer a courtesy minibus service is in operation
- Map F4
- 0935 680 036/ 687 667
- Open 9am–6pm daily
- Adm €10.00
- www.villaromanadel casale.it

Top 10 Features

1. Narthex of the Thermae
2. Private Changing Room for the Thermae
3. Public Room off the Peristyle
4. Great Hunting Scene
5. Ten Girls in Bikinis
6. Xystus
7. Triclinium
8. Arion and Naiads
9. Private Apartments
10. Aqueduct

Narthex of the Thermae

The long narthex in the *thermae* (gym) is decorated with a circus scene *(above)*. Horse-drawn chariots careen around a track, in the centre of which is an image of the obelisk of Constantinus II.

Private Changing Room for the Thermae

Here the emperor's family is shown: mother, son and daughter, accompanied by their slaves, are carrying equipment they will need for the baths and gym *(right)*.

Public Room off the Peristyle

The reception room is decorated with a hunting scene – one of the earliest mosaics laid down in the villa. Hunters and their dogs chase beasts, finally spearing a wild boar, carting him away on their shoulders.

Great Hunting Scene
These mosaics show two countries (personified at either end) surrounded by sea. The array of animals on land (*above*) and in the sea is astounding – including elephants, lions and tigers, and a leopard attacking a gazelle.

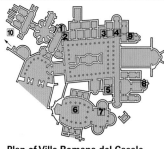

Plan of Villa Romana del Casale

Xystus
On the north side of the *xystus*, the elliptical garden off the *triclinium* (*left*), are three rooms decorated with scenes of the *vendemmia* (grape harvest); the rooms on the south side are decorated with fishing scenes.

Private Apartments
The floors of the family's private apartments are decorated with scenes of a children's hunt. Lush decorative panels throughout depict foliage and baskets of fruit and vegetables.

Aqueduct
Near the entrance to the villa, notice remains of the aqueduct, which provided ample water not only for the baths but also for the extensive gardens, fountains and household use.

Ten Girls in Bikinis
Perhaps the most famous mosaics in the villa (*below*). The bikini-clad athletes have apparently just finished a competition and the winner has been awarded a flowered crown and a palm sceptre.

Triclinium
The triclinium, used for banqueting, opens on one side onto a lovely garden surrounded by an elliptical portico. The mosaics (*above*) are of a grand scale, in keeping with their subject, the Ten Labours of Hercules.

Arion and Naiads
The floor of this living room, which had marble-faced walls, is decorated with a lively scene of the bejewelled Arion playing a lyre. She is surrounded by Naiads and sea creatures, all in fine detail.

Mosaics
The Villa Romana's mosaic floors are almost perfectly preserved because the house was buried under a mudslide in the 12th century. The mosaic artist (possibly North African) was extremely skilled in his craft, assembling millions of tiny polychrome tiles (*tesserae*) to form large-scale images to completely cover more than 3,500 sq m (37,670 sq ft) of floor space. Usually only the most important rooms of the house were decorated, with a flat geometric border and perhaps one small image in the centre of a room.

🔟 Agrigento and the Valle dei Templi

Aligned with Syracuse, Greek Akragas took part in defeating the Carthaginians at Himera in 480 BC. The town boasted a population of around 200,000, constructed temples to its gods, and was known for breeding horses, with which it consistently won the Olympic Games. After being besieged by the Carthaginians in 406 BC, the town was taken by the Romans in 261 BC, renamed Agrigentum, and remained in Roman control until the fall of the Empire. Subsequent versions of Agrigento were built above the acropolis of the ancient city, now known as the Valle dei Templi (Valley of the Temples). Views of the ruins, set on rugged landscape and backed by the sea, are an unmissable sight.

Gigante, Temple of Olympian Zeus

🍴 Avoid the crowded restaurants at the temple site and have a meal in town *(see p115).*

👁 The view of the temples is particularly spectacular at night, when they are floodlit.

• Map D4
• Valle dei Templi: 0922 621 611; Open 8:30am–7pm daily; Adm €10.00
• Archaeological Museum: Contrada S. Nicola 12; 0922 401 565; Open 9am–7pm Tue–Sat, 9am–1pm Mon, Sun & hols; Adm €8.00
• Combined ticket €13.50
• www.parcodeitempli.net

Top 10 Sights
1 Centro Storico
2 Abbazia di Santo Spirito
3 Temple of Herakles
4 Temple of Concord
5 Temple of Hera
6 Temple of Olympian Zeus
7 Sanctuary of the Chthonic Deities
8 Greek Roads, Gates & Walls
9 San Nicola
🔟 Hellenistic/Roman Quarter

1 Centro Storico
Pass through the historic centre to get to the Duomo, walking up from Via Atenea via alleyways *(above)* and passing artisans' workshops and women pausing from their daily chores to chat.

2 Abbazia di Santo Spirito
The abbey *(right)* dates from around 1290 and the resident Cistercian nuns still practise the centuries-old tradition of pastry-making, which was once the exclusive work of the convents.

3 Temple of Herakles
Amid olive and almond trees lie the ruins of this hexastyle temple dating from around 500 BC. It is the oldest of the temples still standing in Agrigento. Cross over the ancient street and walk over the stones to see the parts of the *cella* wall and Doric columns – particularly beautiful at sunset.

At Abbazia di Santo Spirito you can buy a selection of their home-made biscuits with almonds and pistachios.

Temple of Concord

The hexastyle Temple of Concord *(above and below)* remains intact because it was usurped for use as a church. It dates from 430 BC.

Sanctuary of the Chthonic Deities

There are various jumbled remains of what was the walled sanctuary of the underground earth goddesses Demeter and her daughter Persephone.

Map of Agrigento and the Valle dei Templi

San Nicola

The front of the church has an interesting 13th-century portal that incorporates materials from a Roman ruin, and a nicely arched interior in plain stone.

Hellenistic/ Roman Quarter

Among knee-high ruins make out basins, columns, door jambs in walls, mills, steps, remains of the elaborate drainage system, and mosaic flooring in geometric designs.

Temple of Hera

Patches of red at this temple to the queen of the gods (c.450 BC) indicate fire damage, perhaps from the Carthaginian siege of 406 BC.

Temple of Olympian Zeus

This jumble of massive stones *(below)* is all that remains of what was the largest known Greek temple in the world.

Greek Roads, Gates & Walls

Walking from temple to temple throughout the valley, one can see what is left of the infrastructure of the Greek city: roads with ruts, and city walls *(above)* bearing the marks from later ages, when gaps were carved into them to make room for new Byzantine tombs and gates.

Valle dei Templi Guide

The site is divided into three distinct sections, all of which are near a central car park with ticket booth and tourist information office. The Temple of the Olympian Zeus and the Sanctuary of the Chthonic Deities are in an area just to the west of the car park. The entrance to the temples along the Via Sacra (Herakles, Hera and Concord) is just across the street. Just up the Via dei Templi towards town are the museum entrance *(see pp28–9)* to the left and and the entrance to the Hellenistic/Roman Quarter on the right.

In February, when the almond trees are in bloom, the temples are even more picturesque. Come for the Almond Blossom Festival.

Left **Roman Quarter mosaic** Right **Sarcophagus of a child**

Archaeological Museum Exhibits

1 Head of a Bull
Materials excavated from both Agrigento and Gela are found in the first two galleries. They include Bronze Age pots painted with red geometric designs, locally produced pottery, as well as Greek finds. One of the most interesting is the little head of a bull, hand-moulded in pinched terracotta.

2 Vase Collection
The vase collection includes outstanding examples of Attic black-figure and red-figure vases as well as Hellenistic vases. The *krater* (a tall vase with a sturdy base and two handles), with a rare white background, shows the figures of Perseus and Andromeda.

3 Lion-Head Waterspouts
Recovered from various temples at Agrigento (including the Temples of Herakles and Demeter), these spouts, shaped like lions' heads, were originally placed along the roof of temples, just above the cornice, to funnel rainwater to the ground. Note that they were painted in bright colours, as were all of the elements of the temple above the level of the column capitals.

4 Temple of Olympian Zeus Model
This reconstruction of the largest known Greek temple *(see p27)* helps us understand its once enormous size. Note the position of the 8-m- (26-ft-) tall *telamoni* (giant stone figures) in relation to the massive columns. More than twice as tall, the temple's columns measured 16.5 m (54 ft) and had a diameter of 4 m (13 ft) at their base.

5 Telamone and Telamone Heads
Thirty-eight *telamoni* once supported the entablature of the Temple of Olympian Zeus.

Vase collection

A complete figure was reconstructed in the 1800s from various parts found on the site. Each figure was composed of several stones, covered with a smooth stucco overlay, and probably colour as well. Scholars still debate the exact form and position of the *telamoni*, but it may be that they stood with feet splayed.

Ephebus of Agrigento

Described as an *Ephebus* (a youth taking part in a religious rite), this beautifully carved marble figure illustrates the transition from the static archaic style to the severe style. Note the fine modelling of the boy's musculature and the movement of the figure, which dramatically contrasts to the almost Egyptian-like stilted and stiff figures of the former archaic style.

Roman Quarter Mosaics

These particularly fine Roman mosaics from the 2nd century AD are made of tiny *tesserae* (tiles). They served as centrepieces to the decorative mosaic flooring of houses in the residential sector of the city.

Sarcophagus of a Child

Dating from the 2nd century BC, this sarcophagus was only discovered in the 1970s. The panels, carved in high relief, illustrate scenes from the child's life and a detailed scene of the sick room, with the father pulling his beard in mourning.

Greek and Roman Helmets

Found in Eraclea Minoa, the fascinating Greek battle helmets are designed with

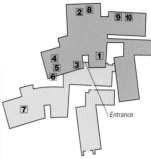

Archaeological Museum Floorplan

ear holes, while the Roman ones have a topknot and finely chased rims.

Red-figure Krater

The "Battle of the Amazons" (c.460 BC) design on this striking *krater* vase has been attributed to the Niobid painter. The artist skilfully created space on the curved surface by illustrating fallen bodies, bows and arrows, and other battlefield paraphernalia in rough perspective. The main scene shows Achilles killing an Amazon queen (and falling in love with her as he does so).

Telamone

⁞10 Selinunte

The ruins of ancient Selinunte (Selinus), once a large settlement at the westernmost reaches of Magna Graecia, loom high on a promontory above the sparkling Mediterranean. Now one of the most important archaeological sites in Europe, it boasts one of the largest Greek temples in the world. Selinunte was founded around 608 BC and enjoyed centuries of prosperity before being reduced to rubble by the Carthaginians during the First Punic War. The city was later totally abandoned (see p33), but its solid yet graceful Doric temples stand out against the bright-blue sky, offering a glimpse of its former grandeur.

Acropolis ruins

🧭 A stunning view of the ruins can be had if you swim out from the beach at Marinella and look to your right.

🅾 The tourist office at Castelvetrano organizes tours of the site in electric carts. Enjoy a picnic dinner amid the ruins while watching ancient myths, classical dance or modern music. Check at the ticket booth for details of live performances.

• Marinella di Selinunte, SS 115 south of Castelvetrano
• Map B4
• 0924 46 277
• Open 9am–6pm (to 4pm in winter; purchase tickets by 4pm)
• Adm €6.00

Top 10 Sights

1 East Group of Temples
2 Temple G
3 Fortified Acropolis Walls
4 Acropolis
5 Temples A and O
6 Temple C
7 Commercial Area and Stoa
8 North Gate
9 Sanctuary of Malophorus
10 Metopes

1 East Group of Temples

Here lie the ruins of three temples on which decorative fragments are identifiable. Re-erected in modern times, Temple E is an example of balanced Doric order.

2 Temple G

The only octastyle temple at Selinunte (all others are hexastyle), Temple G *(above)* is one of the four largest Greek temples in the world. Its columns alone are more than 16 m (52 ft) high. It was left unfinished in 480 BC – note some unfluted columns.

3 Fortified Acropolis Walls

The original walls, built of large blocks of stone, were reinforced after the city was sacked by Carthage in 409 BC, and a second circle built around 305 BC.

4 Acropolis

The promontory was levelled by the first settlers, allowing them to build sacred buildings; commercial and residential structures followed.

5 Temples A and O

Temple A and its twin, Temple O, of which only the base remains, were built in Doric style around 480 BC, making them the most recent ruins on the site.

Temple C
6 Built on a rise, this was the most important temple *(above)*. It was decorated with polychrome stone and terracotta elements.

Plan of Selinunte

Sanctuary of Malophorus
9 This funerary sanctuary dedicated to Malophorus, the pomegranate-bearing goddess, was in use from the 7th to the 3rd centuries BC.

Metopes
10 Selinunte's *metopes* with scenes from Greek mythology are now found in the Archaeological Museum in Palermo *(see p82)*. The carved *metopes* from Temples E and F are outstanding examples of Classical style.

Selinunte Orientation

Selinunte was built on hilltops around the mouths of the Cotone and Selinon (now Modione) rivers. From the main car park, with ticket booth, a path leads to the East Group of Temples. The Acropolis is located across the valley (location of the old harbour) and is accessible on foot or by car; the second car park is at its base. The sanctuary of Malophorus, reached by walking west from the Acropolis, is not accessible to private vehicles. The large residential section of Selinunte lies to the north of the Acropolis but it is not open to the general public.

North Gate
8 Of great importance for the defence of Selinunte, the 7-m- (23-ft-) high North Gate *(below)* was protected by a sophisticated fortification composed of three bastions and a double line of walls. After sustaining damage in 409 BC, the earlier ring of walls was reinforced.

Commercial Area and Stoa
7 Behind Temple D you can see remains of shops, each with two rooms, a courtyard and stairs that led to the shop-keepers' apartments on the upper floors. At the east corner are remains of a *stoa*, or colonnaded marketplace *(above)*.

Left **Temple E, Selinunte** Right **Pediment**

Features of a Doric Temple

1 Proportion
Greek architecture followed rules of proportion to ensure the beauty and harmony of the finished structure. Doric temples were built with a length to width ratio of 3:1 or 2:1. Column height was related proportionally to base diameter, with columns gradually becoming more slender over the centuries.

2 Columns
Doric columns are comprised of a simple capital and a fluted shaft without a base. The shaft is larger in diameter at the bottom than at the top, swelling out slightly in the middle *(entasis)*.

3 Colonnade
Columns are arranged around the outer edge of the temple's *crepidoma* (base), forming a colonnade. "Peripteral" refers to a single colonnade and "dipteral" to a double colonnade.

4 Entablature
The entablature rests above the capitals and below the pediment.

5 Frieze
This is the decorative feature of the entablature. It is made up of alternating triglyphs – grooved blocks ending in little teeth *(guttae)* – which support the structure

above and *metopes* (broad panels usually carved with figurative scenes).

6 Pediments
Pediments are the triangular gables above the entablature on a temple's short sides, usually decorated with polychrome terracotta figures, reliefs or freestanding sculptures.

7 Roof
Roofs were made of wooden beams and terracotta tiles, with polychrome decorations such as gargoyles cast into the shapes of animals' heads which functioned as waterspouts.

8 Colour
Sculpted pieces and architectural elements, particularly the parts of the entablature and the pediment, were always painted in bright colours – most typically in red, blue, white or yellow.

9 Cella
Each temple housed a sanctuary *(cella)*, which was usually an enclosed room in the centre of the temple. Here the sacred image or statue of a god was kept.

10 Altar
A carved block of stone used for animal sacrifices was placed outside temples at the eastern end.

Entablature and column

32

All of the finds from Selinunte can now be seen in Palermo, apart from the Efebo which is now in Castelvetrano.

Top 10 Finds from Selinunte

The Rise and Fall of Selinus

The 80,000 inhabitants of Selinus, named for the abundant wild celery (selinon) which still grows in the area, enjoyed prosperity and power with a sprawling urban complex, impressive temple compounds, their own mint and extensive agricultural holdings. Located on the edge of Greek territory, Selinus was forced to fight border wars with Segesta and was in constant danger from attack by their mighty Carthaginian allies. Although it gradually accepted some Carthaginian influence and even declared itself neutral in the Battle of Himera (480 BC) between the warring Carthaginians and Syracusan Greeks, it preferred to remain a Greek ally. Selinus lost that right in 409 BC, when Hannibal and his forces sacked the town, forcing all inhabitants to abandon the residential sector. From then until its demise, Selinus was restricted to the refortified Acropolis and remained under Punic control. Selinus was finally abandoned in 250 BC, when Carthage, fighting Rome during the First Punic Wars, moved all residents to its stronghold at Lilybaeum (modern-day Marsala). A small community was located at Selinus during the Christian era, but it too was eventually abandoned and all knowledge of the town, even its name, was lost until archaeologists uncovered it in the 19th century.

Rediscovering Selinunte

Archaeological excavations, begun in the 1820s, continue today. In the ruins of the many temples, various architectural elements survive *(left)*, illustrating the one-time might of the city.

Hannibal sacking Selinus

Following pages: **Temple at Segesta (see p91)**

33

Left **The 1968 earthquake devastation** Right **Giuseppe Garibaldi**

Top 10 Moments in History

Ducetius
In what was the last resistance effort against the Greeks, Ducetius unified his people, the Sicels of eastern Sicily, in 452 BC. He succeeded in fortifying positions and redistributing land until suffering final defeat at the hands of Syracuse.

Supremacy of Syracuse
The Syracusan tyrants Heiron I, Gelon, and Dionysus I assured the ascendancy of Greek Sicily, with Syracuse at the helm. The Greek colonies continued to fight among themselves, but united when necessary, including the defeat of the Carthaginians at Himera in 480 BC, calling a halt to 50 years of Carthaginian aggression.

Roman Rule
Rome's successful siege of Syracuse in 212 BC marked the end of Greek power on the island. After centuries of warfare, Roman rule brought peace. *Praetors* were sent to Sicily to govern, including the infamous

Roman invasion

Verres, later prosecuted by Cicero for his misdeeds. Verres, who looted everything from Sicilian wheat to works of art, was the first in a long line of foreign plunderers.

Arab Invasion
After three centuries of long-distance Byzantine rule, North African Moors invaded in AD 827 at Mazara del Vallo. Four years later they took Palermo, made it their capital and transformed it into the cosmopolitan city it remains today. They brought infrastructure to rural Sicily, improved irrigation and introduced new methods of agriculture and fishing.

Count Roger
Norman crusader Roger de Hautville (also known as Count Roger or Roger I) took Sicily at the end of the 11th century. He was the first of a century of Norman rulers who slowly changed Sicily from an eastern to a western society, albeit one with exotic flair *(see p9)*.

The Sicilian Vespers
Having been ruled for decades by the French Angevins, on Easter Monday 1282 an uprising began in Palermo. Using the excuse that a French soldier had insulted a woman, Sicilians killed every Frenchman on the island. Having successfully instigated revolt and done away with the unpopular foreign

sovereign, Sicilians invited Peter of Aragón to become their king. Spanish domination lasted on the island for 500 years.

7 Unification

Centuries of foreign domination, misrule and the feudal system meant wealth, power and land fell into the hands of the few. Popular revolts began in 1820, reached a head in 1848, and in May 1860 opened the way for the Italian socialist Garibaldi. With the aid of Sicilian Redshirts, Garibaldi took the island and convinced the peasant class to vote for Italian Unification.

8 Emigration

After Unification, however, Sicily found itself highly taxed and ignored as an outpost of a "foreign" government. Peasant farmers found themselves unable to feed their families and there was no means for improvement. Such poverty became the motivating factor for mass emigration to the Americas in the late 1800s and early 1900s.

9 Earthquakes

In 1908 an earthquake killed over 70,000 people and levelled more than 90 per cent of Messina. Another devastating quake, in 1968, left scores of villages destroyed in the Belice valley. Thousands were housed in shelters for 15 years, waiting for the government to resolve the problem.

10 Mafia Crackdown

More than 350 *mafiosi* were convicted during the late 1980s, as a result of which the judges Giovanni Falcone and Paolo Borsellino were murdered in 1992. "Boss of Bosses" Salvatore "Totò" Riina was finally convicted of arranging the murders.

Top 10 Mythological Figures

1 Aeneas
Aeneas fled Troy, found refuge on Sicily, and founded Erice and Segesta.

2 Demeter
Goddess of agriculture, the harvest and fertility. Her cult was based at Enna.

3 Persephone
Demeter's daughter was abducted by Hades into the Underworld at Lake Pergusa.

4 Hephaestus (Vulcan)
The god of fire lived on Mount Etna, forging his father Zeus's lightning bolts with the flames of the volcano.

5 Odysseus (Ulysses)
The Greek military leader wandered the Mediterranean for 10 years trying to get home. Many of his adventures took place on Sicily.

6 Polyphemus
The giant one-eyed Cyclops shepherd and cannibal held Odysseus hostage in his Mount Etna cave.

7 Aeolios
The King of the Winds and master of navigation lived on the Aeolian Islands.

8 Arethusa
Chased by the river god Alpheus, Arethusa threw herself into the Ionian sea and sprung up at Syracuse, transformed into a fountain.

9 Acis
Murdered by the jealous Polyphemus, Acis was reincarnated into a river and gave his name to nine towns on the Ionian coast.

10 Scylla & Charybdis
These hideous sea monsters dwelled on either side of the Straits of Messina, terrorizing passing sailors.

Left **Museo Regionale Archeologico, Agrigento** Right **Museo Archeologico Regionale, Syracuse**

TOP 10 Museums

1 Museo Archeologico Regionale "Paolo Orsi", Syracuse

One of the most important archaeological museums in Sicily documents the ancient cultures and civilizations of both the city of Syracuse and eastern Sicily *(see pp20–21)*.

2 Museo Regionale Archeologico, Agrigento

Extensive collections of archaeological finds from Agrigento and related cities reveal the Bronze Age through to Hellenization and the Roman age *(see pp28–9)*.

3 Museo Mandralisca, Cefalù

The museum contains archaeological findings, including ancient Greek and Arab vases, and an art gallery with works mainly by Sicilian artists. Antonello da Messina's *Portrait of a Man* (1465) is housed here.
🔊 *Via Mandralisca 13, Cefalù • Map E2*
• 0921 421 547 • Open 9am–7pm daily
• Adm • www.fondazionemandralisca.it

4 Museo Regionale di Messina

This museum is home to architectural, sculptural and decorative fragments recovered from the city's churches after the 1908 earthquake, as well as paintings and sculpture. Highlights include two works painted by Caravaggio during his stay in Messina in 1608–9: *The Raising of Lazarus* and *The Adoration of the Shepherds*

with dramatically lit, monumental figures. 🔊 *Viale della Libertà 465, Messina • Map H2 • 090 361 292*
• Open 9am–1:30pm daily, 4–6:30pm Tue, Thu, Sat • Adm

5 Museo Archeologico Regionale A. Salinas, Palermo

Objects recovered from sites throughout western Sicily illustrate the development of art and culture from prehistoric eras to the Roman period. 🔊 *Piazza Olivella 24, Palermo • Map L3 • 091 611 6805/6/7*
• Open 9am–1:15pm daily, 3–6:15pm Mon–Fri • Adm

6 Galleria Regionale di Sicilia, Palazzo Abatellis, Palermo

The Catalan-Gothic palace was built at the end of the 15th century and is now home to the collections of the former National Museum. Paintings and sculpture by Sicilian masters span the 13th to 16th centuries, complemented by fine works by Italian and Flemish artists *(see p82)*.

Palazzo Abatellis, Palermo

Museo del Sale, Trapani

Museo del Sale, Trapani
Housed in a restored windmill, exhibits here trace each fascinating stage of traditional salt-making, from filling the saltpans with seawater, to evaporation, recovering, storing, cleaning and grinding the salt *(see p94)*.

Aeolian Archaeological Museum, Lipari
Objects on display in this interesting museum range from obsidian tools of the Neolithic period to items acquired through foreign trade, such as Etruscan red-glazed ceramics. There are also beautiful vases and masks from Greece that have survived from Sicily's Greek occupation *(see p12)*.

Le Ciminiere, Catania
Literally "the chimneys", this former sulphur works has been transformed into a lively cultural centre. Permanent features include the Museo dello Sbarco, a moving reminder of the US and British landings in Sicily in 1943, a cinema museum and a traditional Sicilian puppet theatre. Events and temporary exhibitions are held here, and there is also a restaurant. ◎ *Viale Africa, Catania • Map G4 • 095 401 1928 • Museums open 10am–5pm Tue–Sun (9am–4pm in winter) • Adm*

Casa-Museo di Antonino Uccello, Palazzolo Acreide
The mission of Antonino Uccello was to preserve what he saw as the fast-disappearing culture of peasant farmers. Every item used in the home, workroom, farm, for transportation, entertainment or devotion, was traditionally handmade. The exhibits include puppets, decorated carts, the living quarters of a peasant home and elegantly crafted tools, illustrating a very personal and unique aspect of Sicilian history *(see p123)*.

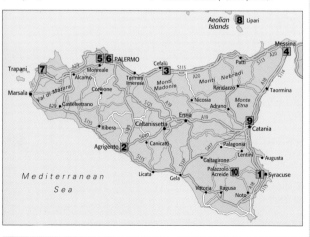

Left **Temple columns, Selinunte** Right **Mosaic, Villa Romana del Casale**

🔟 Ancient Sites

Taormina
Sited in a spectacular position on Monte Tauro, the 3rd-century-BC Greek theatre at Taormina is the second largest in Sicily, but ranks first for the beauty of its backdrop. The view of Reggio di Calabria, the Ionian Sea and Mount Etna is broken only by the *scena* added later by the Romans – perhaps the marble-faced niches and columns were built because the view distracted spectators from any drama on the stage (see pp14–15).

Syracuse
The Greeks founded a colony here in 733 BC and immediately began a programme of development and expansion that led Syracuse to become the most powerful city in the Mediterranean. Rich remains of defensive structures and sacred, social and residential areas are visible today within the modern city and in the surrounding area. A comprehensive archaeology museum makes sense of the varied ruins (see pp18–21).

Villa Romana del Casale
The remains of a luxury hunting villa of a Roman official are the site of the best extant Roman mosaic cycle in the world. The rich figurative and decorative designs adorn the floors of the villa, which is situated in what was a forested area along the road from Catania to Agrigentum (see pp24–5).

Agrigento
In the grounds of the famous Valle dei Templi lie wonderful Greek temples, and an important sanctuary to the goddesses Demeter and Persephone, the so-called Rock Sanctuary and the oldest at Agrigento. Now almost buried by the ugly mass of modern development is the medieval centre of the town, into which fascinating pieces of Greek structures were incorporated (see pp26–9).

Selinunte
The evocative ruins of the residential and commercial sectors and monumental sacred structures are enclosed within the largest archaeological park in Europe. The site protects the ruins of eight massive temples, including one of the largest known temples of the ancient world, Temple C. There are also

Temple of Hera, Agrigento

visible remains of buildings left by the Phoenicians, Greeks, Carthaginians and a Byzantine settlement *(see pp30–33)*.

Segesta
This peaceful and beautiful site comprises the ruins of one of the most important cities of the Elimi, the Hellenized Sicani peoples, and one of the most perfect Doric temples ever constructed. The temple's purpose is unknown, adding further mystery to the already ethereal site – historians debate whether it was built to impress the Greeks in order to gain their military support, or whether it was to decorate a sacred site *(see p91)*.

Solunto
This village was under Carthaginian control, along with Motya and Palermo, until it was taken by the Romans around 250 BC. The grid pattern of the urban plan clearly remains and the paved streets are lined with residences and shops, some well preserved with traces of wall decoration, floor mosaics, steps, columns and cisterns. The latter were of supreme importance because Solunto's position on a promontory above the Tyrrhenian Sea did not offer any natural water sources *(see p94)*.

Morgantina
Morgantina was an important commercial centre along the trade route from the north coast of Sicily and the Aeolian Islands to the south, and extensive ancient remains have recently been excavated here. Deep in Sicani and Sicel territory, the city flourished during the Hellenistic and Roman periods, and most of the ruins date from that time *(see p110)*.

Motya

Motya
The island city in the lagoon between Marsala and Trapani was used from the 8th century BC by the Phoenicians as a base for controlling shipping routes in the eastern Mediterranean. It became a Carthaginian stronghold until its complete destruction by Syracuse in 397 BC. Today, the small island is covered with remains of that great city – walls with fortified gates and towers surround the entire perimeter and there is a manmade harbour within the walls. Ancient paved roads and sacred and residential areas can also be clearly seen *(see p92)*.

Tindari
The ruins of ancient Tyndaris are remarkably well preserved. This was one of the last Greek colonies in Sicily, founded by the Syracusans in 396 BC. Features include the remains of a Roman villa and baths, as well as a splendid amphitheatre facing the sea. There is also a sanctuary with a Black Madonna, to which a pilgrimage is made every 8 September. Magnificent views from the Promontory of Tyndaris include the beautiful Laguna di Oliveri *(see p101)*.

Left **Pasta** Right *Fico d'India* cactus plants

🔟 Vestiges of Invading Powers

Sicilian Dialect
It's not an accent but a language of its own. Like Sicily itself, the dialect is a palimpsest created from foreign invasions and sounds like the exotic mix it is: a Romance language with influences of Italian, Arabic, Latin, Greek, French, Spanish, Lombard, Ligurian and English. Reflecting the fatalism of the populace, it has no future tense.

Pasta
Fresh pasta, made of regular wheat flour, was made in Italy as early as the Etruscan era. Dried pasta, which can be stored, was most likely invented by the Arabs using Sicily's *semola*, a hard durum wheat flour.

Place Names
Many place names are Italian versions of original Greek or Latin names. Erice was known as Monte San Giuliano until 1934, when Mussolini went on a name-changing spree and adopted an Italian version of its original Greek name, Eryx. Arabic names remain in abundance – look for names with the prefixes "Calta", "Gibil" and "Sala".

Urban Plans
Urban plans of modern towns often follow ancient street patterns. The area of narrow straight streets known as *la pettina* (the comb) in Syracuse is left over from the Greeks. The tiny, winding streets of Palermo's old neighbourhoods such as La Kalsa, or the street plan of Castelvetrano, come from Arab settlements. Cefalù's system of parallel streets leading down to the sea is Norman.

Fishing Techniques
Sicily's now famous fishing techniques were adapted from Arabic methods. Tuna fishermen still practise the *mattanza* in the channel between Levanzo and Favignana, encouraging tuna through a system of nets until the final so-called "chamber of death", where they are brought close to the surface to be slaughtered. Fishermen work together chanting rhythmically to haul them aboard and to shore. Near Messina, swordfish are hunted from boats called *feluche*. The swordfish are spotted from the tall mast and harpooned from a long plank extending from the prow.

Mattanza tuna fishermen

Sicilian lemon trees

Crops
6 The Spanish introduced tomatoes, potatoes, chocolate and the prickly-pear cactus, or *fico d'India*; the Greeks introduced olive trees and grapevines; the Arabs brought citrus fruits, sugar cane, date palms, pistachios, flax, cotton and mulberries.

Fortified Towers
7 The Spanish protected Sicily's coastline with more than 100 defensive towers. Messages were passed from one to the other by fire signals.

Waterworks
8 Greeks and Romans used aqueducts and water-powered mills, while Arabs introduced land irrigation.

Erosion
9 The Romans began deforestation of the island to export timber and make way for wheat plantations. Sicily is now virtually treeless and the earth is easily washed away in heavy rains.

Latifondi
10 The system of single-owner wheat farms *(latifondi)* was codified by the Normans, so by the 1880s farmers had to compete for minuscule plots of land, resulting in mass poverty and, eventually, mass immigration.

Top 10 Invaders

1 Greeks
The first Greek colony founded at Naxos in 734 BC displaced Sicel inhabitants.

2 Carthaginians
Carthage invaded repeatedly and many Punic War battles were fought on Sicily.

3 Romans
After years of warfare, Rome finally took Sicily after the fall of Syracuse in 212 BC.

4 Byzantines
In AD 535 Sicily became part of Justinian's Eastern Roman Empire.

5 Arabs
The Arab conquest of the island began in AD 827 and was complete only in AD 902 with the fall of Taormina.

6 Normans
After 30 years of crusades, Count Roger de Hautville took Sicily in 1091 (see p36).

7 Spaniards
Peter of Aragón was crowned King of Sicily in 1282, beginning 440 years of Spanish domination.

8 Bourbons
Sicily was given to the House of Savoy in the 1713 Peace of Utrecht treaty, and swapped for Sardinia seven years later, thereby coming under Habsburg rule.

9 Italians
Garibaldi and his Red Shirts invaded at Marsala in 1860, starting the campaign that ended with the Unification of Italy.

10 Allied Forces
On 10 July 1943, Allied Forces under generals Patton and Montgomery landed at Licata and Pachino, taking Sicily in 38 days (see p39, Le Ciminiere).

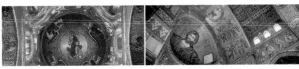

Left **La Martorana** Right **Monreale**

🔟 Places of Worship

1 Monreale

The monastery and Church of Santa Maria La Nova were founded by William II in 1174. His tomb, along with the tombs of his family members, including his father, King William I, and mother, Queen Margaret, are in the south transept *(see pp10–11)*.

2 Cappella Palatina, Palermo

This masterpiece of Arab-Norman art celebrates both the Glory of God and Norman rule. Masses are said in the richly decorated chapel *(see p8)*.

3 San Domenico, Palermo

The "Pantheon" of Palermo is so-called because Sicily's most illustrious citizens are buried here. Among them are the physicist Stanislao Cannizzaro, the parliamentarian Ruggero Settimo, the painter Pietro Novelli, and other members of the nobility *(see p81)*.

4 Cathedral, Cefalù

In 1131, after several days on stormy seas, Norman King Roger II landed safely at Cefalù and, giving thanks to God, endowed a bishopric and commissioned the cathedral now famous for its Byzantine mosaic decoration and its beautifully restored cloisters. In a piazza surrounded by tall palms, the church with its two typically Norman square bell towers is backed by Cefalù's dramatic rocky crag *(see p99)*. ◈ *Piazza Duomo • Map E2 • 0921 922 021 • Ring*

for admittance (opening times change monthly) • Free (adm to cloisters)

5 La Martorana, Palermo

The only original part of the exterior of this 1143 Norman masterpiece is its splendid bell tower, now minus its red dome. Among its splendid mosaics is the only known portrait of King Roger II *(see p81)*.

6 Cathedral, Syracuse

The Catholic Church often chose sites sacred to other cults on which to construct their places of worship, but this one is unique for being set within a previous site. Behind the Baroque façade, the structure of a Greek temple to Athena has been adapted for use as a church. ◈ *Piazza Duomo • Map H5 • Open 7:30am–8pm daily • Adm*

Cefalù Cathedral

Mass is often held at intervals throughout the day; tourists are not permitted to tour churches during services.

San Nicola, Agrigento

San Nicola, Agrigento

The 13th-century church is located within the Valle dei Templi, and its façade incorporates Gothic motifs with ancient Roman columns. The interior was renovated in the early 1300s and the early 1400s. In a chapel on the right, there is an interesting Roman sarcophagus decorated with reliefs of Greek mythology (see p27). ◎ Piazza Duomo • Map D4 • Open for weddings only • Free

San Carlo al Corso, Noto

Dedicated to San Carlo Borromeo, this church is on the Corso and forms part of Noto's dramatic Baroque skyline. Climb the bell tower for fantastic views of the city's Baroque architecture (see pp22–3). ◎ Corso Vittorio Emanuele • Map G5 • Open 9am–noon, 3–7pm daily • Adm (bell tower only)

San Giorgio, Ragusa

The cathedral of Ragusa Ibla is built on a rise in a wide tree-lined piazza in the heart of the old town. The convex, undulating façade is typical of the architect Gagliardi, supporting a soaring central tower, bulging columns and swirly volutes. ◎ Piazza Duomo • Map F5 • Open 9:30am–noon, 4–7pm • Free

Other Faiths, Palermo

Given its long history of invasion (see pp42–3), Sicily has always been a cosmopolitan island, and nowhere more so than in its capital. Palermo is home to places of worship for a number of faiths and includes a mosque – a clear remnant of its former Arab inhabitants.
◎ Mosque: Piazza Gran Cancelliere 6; Opening times vary; Free • Evangelical Church: Via Parlatore Giuseppe 12; Opening times vary; Free • Anglican Church: via Mariano Stabile 118; Opening times vary; Free

Left **Castello di Sperlinga** Right **Castello Eurialo**

🔟 Castles

Castello Eurialo
These 4th-century-BC fortifications protected the western approach to Greek Syracuse. Archimedes refined the structure, adding a drawbridge, trenches and catapults to protect the keep. Descend into one of the defensive trenches where the tunnels give access to the keep *(see p122)*.

Caccamo
This 12th-century Norman castle dominates the village and valley below. Pass through the once impregnable walls, walk among ramparts, and visit the *Sala di Congiura* (Hall of the Conspiracy), where in 1160 the barons plotted to overthrow King William I. ◈ *Caccamo • Map D3 • Open 9am–1pm, 3–7pm Tue-Sun • Adm*

Castello di Venere, Erice
This Norman castle is impressively sited on a sheer cliff face. The entrance through the tower is marked by the coat of arms of Charles V. Inside, the

Castello di Venere

remains of Norman walls surround the ancient area sacred to Venus Erycina – stones from her temple were used to build the castle. There are also Phoenician and Roman ruins here. ◈ *Via Conte Pepoli • Map B2 • Open Apr–Oct: 10am–6pm daily; Nov–Mar: daily (reservation required) • Adm*

Castello di Lombardia, Enna
One of the largest castles in Sicily was built by Frederick II in 1233 on the highest point of the already towering village. Massive walls and defensive works remain, including six of what were once 20 towers. The octagonal Torre di Federico II is the only fully original part remaining. Climb the Torre Pisana for views of the city, the valley below and Mount Etna on the horizon. ◈ *Map E4 • Open 8am–8pm daily • Free*

Aci Castello
The castle is perched atop a black promontory, jutting out over the sea. Built by the Normans, it was covered by lava flows in 1169. It was rebuilt by a traitor to the crown, then partially destroyed by Frederick II of Aragón in 1297. A stairway scales the side of the fortifications, giving access to the interior of the structure. The passages and chambers now hold the archaeological collection of the Museo Civico. ◈ *Map G4 • Open 9am–1pm, 3:30–7pm daily (to 5pm winter) • Adm*

Castello Ursino

6 Castello Ursino, Catania

Built around 1250, the once-moated castle has been used variously as a royal residence, the seat of parliament and a prison. It now houses the town's Museo Civico. ◈ *Piazza Federico di Svevia • Map G4 • Open 9am–1pm daily, 3–7pm Mon–Sat • Adm*

7 Castello Ventimiglia, Castelbuono

In 1316 the Ventimiglia family built their fortified family seat on top of a rocky outcrop in the heart of the Madonie mountains. Within is a Baroque chapel dedicated to Sant'Anna by Giacomo Serpotta (1652–1732). ◈ *Map E3 • Open 9:30am–1pm, 3:30–7pm Tue–Sun • Adm*

8 Castello di Sperlinga

Sperlinga guarded the vital royal Norman supply road linking Palermo with Catania. As the site of the only resistance to the Sicilian Vespers in 1282, a group of Angevins hid out here for over a year. ◈ *Via Castello • Map F3 • Open Apr–Sep: 9am–1:30pm, 3–7pm daily; Oct–Mar: 9am–1pm, 2–6pm daily • Adm*

9 Castello, Lipari

Above the harbour, Lipari's castle rock has been fortified for six millennia. The 12th-century Norman gate offers a passage through walls fortified by the Greeks in the 4th century BC and again by the Spanish in 1556. ◈ *Map G1 • Open 9am–1:30pm, 3–6pm (4–7pm in summer) • Free*

10 Castello di Donnafugata

Donnafugata is a hodge-podge of architectural styles. The Arabs first fortified the site around AD 1000; it then became a castle around 1300. In 1865, it was turned into a far grander building, and a Venetian Gothic loggia was added. ◈ *Map F6 • Open: see www.comune.ragusa.gov.it/turismo/castello/09oraricastello.html • Adm*

Sicily's Top 10

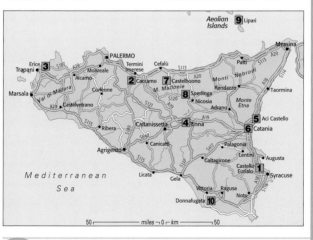

Aeolian Islands — **9** Lipari

Messina

PALERMO — Termini Imerese — Cefalù — S113 — Patti — S113

Erice — **3** — S187 — A29 — Monreale — S113

Trapani

Alcamo

Val di Mazara — A29 — Castelvetrano — Corleone — **2** Caccamo — **7** Castelbuono — A20 — Monti Nebrodi — Randazzo — A19 — Taormina

Marsala

S115

Caltanissetta — S120 — Sperlinga — **8** Nicosia — Adrano — Monte Etna

S121

Ribera — S650 — **4** Enna — A19 — **5** Aci Castello — **6** Catania

Agrigento — Canicattì — S117

Palagonia — S417 — Lentini — Augusta

S115 — Licata — Caltagirone — S194

Gela — Castello Euriolo — **1** Syracuse

Mediterranean Sea

Vittoria — Ragusa — Noto

Donnafugata — **10**

50 |——— miles ⌐ 0 ⌐ km ———| 50

47

Left **Corleone** Right **Petralia Soprana**

🔟 Villages

1 Petralia Soprana
The highest village in Madonie, at 1,147 m (3,760 ft) above sea level, medieval Petralia Soprana feels untouched by the modern world. Narrow alleyways are filled with the aroma of bakers making their traditional cinnamon biscuits, while the vistas of the rolling mountains below are breathtaking. ◈ Map E3

2 Scopello di Sopra
This small village of fishermen was almost inaccessible until recent years, when the road was built from Castellammare. Now the village is experiencing something of a tourist boom, but retains the charm of a tiny fishing hamlet, and you'll still see an old mariner with nets stretched the length of the piazza, repairing the gaps with an enormous needle. ◈ Map C2

3 Poggioreale Vecchio and Poggioreale
In the heart of the Belice Valley, Poggioreale Vecchio (the old town) was founded in 1642 and managed to survive as a self-sufficient village until the earthquake of 1968 left it nothing more than a ghost town. Modern progress arrives slowly in the remote interior, and Poggioreale Vecchio looks much as it did in the 1800s. The people of old Poggioreale who were left homeless after the earthquake moved into a new government-sponsored town 15 years after the event. The new Poggioreale, a 1980s design by Paolo Portoghese, is full of flamboyant architecture, yet sadly filled with rather uninviting public spaces. ◈ Map C3

4 Cefalù
The ancient village was given new life in 1131, when Count Roger founded the cathedral here – its architecture and mosaic decoration make it one of Sicily's must-sees (see p44). Although a constant tourist draw, the village has managed to keep some of its medieval character (see p99).

5 Erice
Erice has managed to maintain much of its medieval charm. The buildings are all built of locally quarried white stone, adding to its storybook appearance. The steep streets

Cefalù

Erice

are also paved in characteristic patterns, the stones worn slick with time *(see p93)*.

Corleone
Made famous by the film *The Godfather*, parts of which were actually filmed in Savoca, in the northeast, Corleone is the largest village in the area. A few 13th-century structures are visible in the centre. ✎ *Map C3*

Palazzo Adriano
In the heart of this fertile area, Palazzo Adriano is lofty and remote. In Piazza Umberto I are two churches, the Catholic Santa Maria del Lume and the Greek

Orthodox Santa Maria Assunta, built by Albanian refugees in the 1400s. Palazzo Adriano was the setting for the film *Cinema Paradiso (see p61)*. ✎ *Map D3*

Novara di Sicilia
This little mountain village is tucked between the Peloritani and Nebrodi mountain ranges. The medieval site has a crumbling Arab castle and the 16th-century Chiesa Madre with naive wood carvings on the altar. ✎ *Map G2*

Palazzolo Acreide
Palazzolo Acreide is a lovely village with an impressive mix of sites – originally Greek, most of what you see today is Baroque, though a Greek theatre still stands. The churches are spectacular, particularly the tiny Church of the Annunciation with its twisting columns. ✎ *Map G5*

Scicli
Rebuilt after the earthquake of 1693, Scicli combines open, tree-lined piazzas, swirling Baroque façades with older structures with terracotta tiled roofs. ✎ *Map F6*

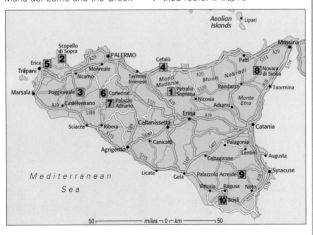

Palazzolo Acreide and Scicli are both UNESCO World Heritage Sites.

Left **Castellammare del Golfo** Right **Selinunte beach**

🔟 Beaches

Selinunte
A large sandy beach stretches to the east of the port and just below the temples *(see pp30–33)*. Bathing establishments offer beach chairs, watersports equipment, restaurants and bars. It tends to be crowded with students showing off their skimpy suits and tans, but through the small pine wood to the west you'll find an open beach for families. ◎ *Map B4*

Castellammare del Golfo
The beaches west of Castellammare are prettier and less populated than those to the east. There are plenty of gorgeous coves with clear water – most spectacular are those with pebble beaches in Lo Zingaro *(see p91)* and at Scopello Tonnara, with its rock towers and old boat ramp for sunbathing. ◎ *Map C2*

Eraclea Minoa
Below the ruins of the Greek city *(see p110)* a little seaside village comes to life in summer. The sandy beach is long, wide and open, and buffered by pine woods. At either end are two bars providing beach chairs and snacks. ◎ *Map C4*

Mazzarò & Giardini-Naxos
The water at the two resorts below Taormina is a calm, brilliant blue. The cable car from Taormina descends to Mazzarò, a developed resort area with two pebble beaches lined with well-equipped bathing establishments, coves for exploring and the popular island of Isola Bella *(see p15)*. Giardini-Naxos is a fully fledged town with a port and long stretches of beach lined with hotels *(see p100)*.

Mondello
This is Palermo's backyard. It is crowded with seaside villas of Palermo's aristocracy and locals of all walks of life taking advantage of the beach, bars, *gelaterie*, restaurants and clubs. For swimming, nature and tranquillity, this may not be the best beach in Sicily, but it's high on the list for those who want to participate in the scene. ◎ *Map D2*

Pollara, Salina
This beach is a crescent of large pebbles with a dramatic cliff backdrop. When the wind is high, Pollara beach disappears under the waves, even at the height of summer. The view out to the sea is dramatic, with a craggy *faraglione* (rock tower)

View of Mazzarò

Mondello

poking up out of the dark sea. As there is little development here, bring food and drink from town or get supplies from the vendor and his friends at the booth set up in the church piazza (see p13).

Scoglitti & Donnalucata
The sandy beaches along this southeast stretch of coast are long and wide and splashed with green-blue surf. There is very little tourist development to speak of, beyond small fishing villages including Scoglitti and Donnalucata, with their nice markets and good restaurants, and little seaside villages that come to life in summer, such as Marina di Ragusa. ◈ Map F6

Lampedusa
The tiny islet Isola dei Conigli, off Lampedusa, and the bay in between have been set apart as a nature reserve for sea turtles who lay their eggs on the beach. The water is clean and shallow in the bay and the sands are white, but there are no facilities, so bring your own supplies. ◈ Map B6

Aci Castello
Here clear, blue water laps onto the black lava rocks just below the castle (see p46). Descend to the left, where a water polo court is set up in summer, or to the right to a wooden deck for sunbathing and diving. ◈ Map G4

Vendicari
A spectacular nature reserve with sandy beaches set around a 15th-century Aragonese tower. The pristine coast here offers a peaceful, natural experience. The park is covered with Mediterranean maquis, and its wetland habitat provides a resting stop for birds migrating to and from Africa. ◈ Map G6

Left **Boating** Right **Sunbathing on a water dinghy**

🔟 Outdoor Activities

The Passeggiata
Walking up and down a city or village's main street is Sicily's supreme activity, allowing for socializing, doing business and people-watching (see p69).

Swimming
The unspoiled, clear water off Sicily and the offshore islands is spectacular, and also great for snorkelling and scuba-diving. The shoreline varies from sandy to pebble beaches, private coves, grottoes and rock formations. Lifeguards are not always on duty, so swim at your own risk (see p137).

Skiing, Mount Etna
The depth of snow depends on underground lava flows that affect surface temperatures, but there's enough of a base for winter-time skiing on the northern slopes. Pick a base at Zafferana Etnea, Nicolosi or Linguaglossa, where ski rentals, a ski school and lifts are available (see pp16–17).

The passeggiata

Golf
Three 18-hole courses are up and running in Sicily, with eight more dramatically sited courses scheduled to open soon. The courses are often part of a luxury hotel complex offering spas, culinary initiatives and cultural events. ⊗ Il Picciolo Golf Club: www.ilpicciologolf.com • Le Madonie Golf Club: www.lemadoniegolf.com • www.italygolfandmore.com • Verdura Golf & Spa Resort: www.verduraresort.com

Hiking
Find great hikes all over the island, whether you're looking for a strenuous climb up a volcano, a long walk through the green hills of the interior or an exciting hike on trails clinging to the cliffs above the blue sea. Most nature reserves are orientata (orientated), meaning that they have marked trails that are usually graded for difficulty. Try Mount Etna, Stromboli or Vulcano, or the gorges of the southeast. Lo Zingaro has a good selection of trails ranging in difficulty, as do the parks of the Nebrodi and Madonie mountain ranges (see p101).

Fishing, Favignana
You can't join in the traditional mattanza fishing ritual, although you can watch it in progress if you happen to be there when the tuna are running (see p42). You can also rent a boat with a local captain for a day's fishing.

Horse riding, Madonie mountains

Horse Riding
7 Nature reserves such as Mount Etna, the Madonie and Nebrodi mountain ranges and Lo Zingaro are populated with small farms that rent horses. Ask at the nearest base hotel or check park literature for *ippoturismo* and *maneggio* (stables).

Cycling
8 All but the most serious cyclists may have a rough time on the steep terrain of much of the island. Cycling is a great way to sightsee in the quieter towns and resorts, however, and many offer free bike rentals through tourist offices. Renting a bicycle on the offshore islands is a convenient way to get around.

Boating
9 Sail your own, arriving at one of Sicily's many ports *(see p130)*, or rent a boat and a captain for an insider's tour of hidden coves.

Water Sports
10 Diving and snorkelling are available with trained guides through diving centres in many places, including Scopello and the Aeolian Islands, or snorkel on your own, taking advantage of the marine life along Sicily's shores. Beaches in more touristy areas rent pedal boats and windsurfing boards.

Top 10 Sicilian Flora and Fauna

1 Sea Turtles
Rare sea turtles bury their eggs in the sands of the Belice Estuary and the Pelagie Islands.

2 Sanfratellano Horse
A species indigenous to the Nebrodi, descendant of the ancient *Equus sicanus*.

3 Birds of Prey
Golden eagles, peregrine falcons and owls hunt in the island's nature reserves.

4 Cactus
The *fico d'India*, or prickly pear, is omnipresent as it thrives in Sicily's arid climate.

5 Dwarf Palm
The tiny palm flourishes in the northwest; its fronds are used by craftsmen for weaving baskets and brooms.

6 Fennel
Bright yellow, fluffy green or tall and crispy brown, depending upon the season, it covers hillsides and springs up along the side of roads.

7 Agave
The low-growing aloe-like plant with curling spiky leaves shoots out a central stalk that can reach up to 12 m (40 ft).

8 Flowering Vines
Growing out of control and perfuming the countryside are jasmine, bougainvillea, honeysuckle and morning glory.

9 Thistle
The hearty, spiky plant pops up along roadsides and in fields with its bright purple flowers – not to be confused with cultivated artichokes.

10 Forests
The few remains of once prevalent pine, oak, cork-oak and beech forests are now carefully protected.

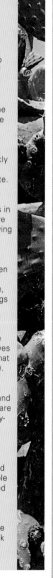

For specialist activity holidays in Sicily See p131

53

Left **Puppets** Right **Museo del Sale**

🔟 Children's Attractions

1 Puppet Theatres
Puppet theatres offer rip-roaring, gory re-enactments of the Norman crusader sword fights, lively music, and encourage the audience to root for a favourite crusader. The puppets "speak" in Italian, or Sicilian dialect, but an English-language written account of the story is often provided by the theatre. In any event, it's easy enough to follow the action without understanding every word *(see pp64–5).*

2 Castles
All of Sicily's invaders needed to defend their position, so they built fortified castles along the coastline and on high points inland to guard the roads and towns. Sicily's countless castles are rich in history and offer plenty of good romping around the ramparts, searching for secret passageways, dungeons, trapdoors, tiny spy windows and hidden places from which the occupants would pour boiling oil down onto the enemy *(see pp46–7).*

Venus Castle, Erice

3 Museo della Lava (MULA), Viagrande
This interactive museum uses 3D models and satellite images to explain volcanic phenomena in a fun and interesting manner. Man's relationship with the volcano is also explored, with special regard to the towns around Etna, which for centuries have been living with the constant threat provided by Europe's largest active volcano *(see pp16–17).* ◈ *Via Dietro Serra 6, Viagrande • Map G3 • 095 789 0768 • Open 9:30am–1:30pm Sun & hols (last entry 12:30pm); by appointment Mon–Sat*

4 Museo del Sale, Paceco
Just south of Trapani, the small museum of salt is located inside a restored windmill. Its fascinating exhibits show how the windmill transfers water from pool to pool and grinds the harvested salt. Work in the salt pans themselves is on-going, and you can see each stage that goes into transforming sea water to table salt. There is a restaurant on site *(see p94).*

5 Museo del Giocattolo, Catania
Catania's child-friendly toy museum displays toys and games dating back to the 1850s. Work-shops and play areas allow kids to join in with games their great-grandparents might have enjoyed as children. ◈ *Piazzale Asia, "Le Ciminiere," Catania • Map G4 • 095 0947 899 • Open 9am–1pm, 3–6:30pm Tue–Fri; 9am–1pm Sat & Sun; closed Aug • Adm*

Aquarium, Syracuse

Aquarium, Syracuse
The Syracuse *Acquario* offers a close look at marine life in the Mediterranean, housed in 40 different tanks. Additional sections are dedicated to fresh-water and tropical habitats. It is located at the Fonte Aretusa, on the island of Ortygia, and entry is from the marina below.
🕭 *Largo Aretusa, Ortygia • Map H5 • Open 10am–8pm daily • Adm*

Motya
The archaeological park on the island of Motya starts and ends with a short boat ride across the lagoon (less than 10 minutes each way). The park itself is wide open, and offers excellent examples to inquisitive kids of how the Phoenicians and then the Carthaginians lived and fortified their villages. In addition to Motya, all of Sicily's archaeo-logical parks offer space to run around and usually ruins to explore *(see p92)*.

Museo Geologico Gemellaro, Palermo
Palermo's impressive geological museum fascinates children and adults alike with displays from its collection of over 600,000 artifacts and specimens. These include remains of the elephants that roamed

Phoenician figure, Motya

Sicily in the Pleistocene era; a quartz crystal containing a drop of Mediterranean seawater over 5 million years old; the skeleton of a woman, known as Thea, dating from the late Stone Age; and rare finds from the volcanic island of Ferdinandea, which has risen and sunk again many times over the centuries, the last sighting being in 1832. 🕭 *Corso Tukori 131, Palermo • Map L6 • 0912 53 9477 • Open 9am–1pm daily (Sat by appt), 3–5pm Mon–Thu • Adm*

Etnaland
Sicily's top theme park has a full-size dinosaur park and all sorts of water rides, including the popular journey over Crocodile Rapids. There are rides gentle enough for the youngest children, and others that will get even the most hardened theme park veter-ans' adrenaline flowing. A more modest water park, Acquasplash, is located near Selinunte. 🕭 *Etna-land, Belpasso; Map G4; 0957 913 334; Open late Jun–early Sep: 9am–7pm daily; www.etnaland.eu; Adm • Acquasplash, Lungomare Est, Tre Fontane, Selinunte; Map B4; www.acquasplash.net; Adm*

Nature Reserves
Sicily's nature reserves are good places to spot wildlife, climb about, picnic and go swimming. Hiking trails are graded for various levels of expertise. Mount Etna *(see pp16–17)* is probably the most fascinating for kids and adults alike – the volcano is always at least smoking, if not throwing red sparks into the air. Guides give a lively account of lava flowing underfoot and the gift shops screen spectacular video footage from past eruptions.

Left **Carnevale, Sciacca** Right **Santa Rosalia celebrations, Palermo**

Festivals

1 Santa Lucia, Syracuse

A procession of a silver statue of Syracuse's patron saint travels from the Duomo to the Chiesa di Santa Lucia, built on the spot where she was martyred in AD 304. As the protector of eyesight, the faithful attach votive eyes made from silver, bronze or wax to her image. 🔊 *13 Dec*

2 San Paolo and San Sebastiano, Palazzolo Acreide

Rivals for centuries, the landowners and farmers loyal to San Paolo and the artisans and merchants loyal to San Sebastiano try to out-celebrate each other. Huge statues of the saints make an entrance from the church into the piazza, where they are met with brightly coloured streamers, then journey through the village. Worshippers process barefoot well into the night. 🔊 *San Paolo: 29 Jun; San Sebastiano: 10 Aug*

Santa Lucia statue, Syracuse

3 Santa Rosalia, Palermo

Rosalia was the daughter of a nobleman but chose a hermitic life in a cave on Monte Pellegrino. The discovery of her relics "saved" Palermo from the plague in 1624. For six days, her relics, atop an ornate *vara* (float), are paraded around the streets of the city. 🔊 *Mid-Jul*

4 San Giuseppe, Belice Valley

St Joseph's Day is celebrated fervently in the west, especially in villages such as Salemi and Poggioreale. Altars are constructed in homes, schools and public spaces, piled high with ornate breads and traditional foods – but no meat, out of respect for St Joseph's poverty. 🔊 *18–19 Mar*

5 Good Friday, Noto

The Holy Thorn is processed through the streets accompanied by the black-veiled Grieving Madonna. The solemn procession is accompanied by a drum and a trumpet, periodically letting out a mournful blast.

6 Festival of the Assumption, Randazzo

One of the most spectacular floats of all the Sicilian festivals is paraded from Piazza di Santa Maria through the narrow streets of the village to Piazza Loreto. The tall float carries young local boys dressed up as angels, saints, Jesus and the Madonna. 🔊 *15 Aug*

Sant'Agata festival, Catania

Sant'Agata, Catania
One of the earliest saints, Agata was martyred in Catania's Piazza Stesicoro. The bejewelled reliquary bust of the saint is paraded around town followed by fanciful golden "candlesticks" so large that each one is hauled on the backs of 10 men. Balconies are draped in fabrics, flags fly, candles burn, and fireworks thunder at dawn. ◈ *Early Feb*

Good Friday, Trapani
A procession of 20 huge scenes of Christ's Passion, decorated with flowers, is accompanied by bands playing funeral dirges.

Easter Sunday, Castelvetrano
Crowds gather in Castelvetrano to see the statue of Christ enter from one end of the piazza, while the Madonna enters from the other. To a dramatic drumbeat, they move toward one another and come together in an embrace.

Carnevale, Sciacca, Termini Imerese, Acireale
The historic streets of these towns are packed with revellers for parades, parties and competitions. *Papier mâché* floats satirize current events or figures of popular culture. ◈ *Feb*

Top 10 Food Festivals

1 Mostra dei Formaggi della Valle del Belice e Sagra della Ricotta, Poggioreale
Watch ricotta made in traditional and modern methods.
◈ *Late May or early Jun*

2 Sagra del Cappero, Pollara, Salina
A caper festival, with local food, music and dancing.
◈ *1st Sun in Jun*

3 Couscous Fest, San Vito lo Capo
Chefs compete in an international couscous contest, with tastings. ◈ *Last week in Sep*

4 Sagra della Ciliegia, Chiusa Sclafani
Cherry festival, with traditional folk music. ◈ *1st or 2nd Sun in Jun*

5 Sagra del Pesce Azzurro, Selinunte
A procession of the Madonna of the Fishermen and a sardine feast. ◈ *Late Aug*

6 Ottobrata Zafferanese
Throughout Zafferana Etnea, a fair of local wine, chestnuts, cheese, honey and mushrooms. ◈ *Every Sun in Oct*

7 Inycon, Menfi
Wine festival with food, music, dance and crafts.
◈ *Late Jun–early Jul*

8 Sagra del Carciofo, Cerda
Artichoke festival, and music in the main piazza. ◈ *25 Apr*

9 Sagra del Carrubo, Frigintini
A tasting of pasta and carob biscuits. ◈ *Oct*

10 Sagra del Pistacchio, Bronte
A lively week-long festival dedicated to the tasty local nut. ◈ *Late Sep–early Oct*

Left **Harvesting olives for olive oil** Right **Grapes for wine-making**

Customs and Traditions

Hand Gestures
A Grand Tour author reported that Sicilians had been using hand gestures since the Greek invasion as a way of furthering resistance against foreign rule. Some of the common gestures you see mean: "She's pretty", "This tastes great", "Let's go", "I couldn't care less", "Do you want to stop for a coffee?", "Be careful", "That's not such a good idea" and "His wife is cheating on him."

Proverbs
No good Sicilian is ever without a witty quip spoken in dialect. Examples include: *Cu' avi 'nna bona vigna, avi pani, vinu e ligna* (He who owns a good vineyard has bread, wine and wood); *Cu nun 'sapi l'arti, chiudi putia* (He who does not know his craft, closes his shop); *Soggira e nora calaru di n'celu sciarriannu*s (Mothers-in-law and daughters-in-law were sent from heaven and started fighting before they hit the ground); and *La soggira voli bene a la nora comu n'rizzu n'pettu* (Mothers-in-law love their daughters-in-law like a sea urchin in bed).

I Morti
The feast of All Souls on 2 November is celebrated to the hilt. Families visit the cemetery, where tombs have been rigorously tidied up and adorned with fresh flowers for the glory of the dead and for approval of family members and anyone else casting a judgmental eye. Relatives from the other world leave gifts for children, such as toys, *frutta martorana* (fake fruits crafted of almond paste) and *pupi di cera*, garishly coloured sugar dolls.

Festivals
Festivals for patron saints once offered the only chance for a holiday, socializing and entertainment. Often celebrated in spring, giving farmers a chance to rest after the planting and to pray for a successful harvest, the *festa* was the one day everyone came in from the fields for religious processions, games, horse races, music and fireworks. Even the *gelato* salesman and puppet theatre came to town. The same festivals are still celebrated as a chance to dress up and get together *(see pp56–7).*

Sicilian festival

5 Legends

King Roger's 12th-century French court poets told stories of Charlemagne and the paladins and the King Arthur cycle which once included Sicily in its milieu: Morgan Le Fay took wounded King Arthur to recover in a cave on Mount Etna. The paladins survive today as puppet theatre heroes *(see pp64–5)* and Morgan Le Fay retained her presence in Sicily as *Fata Morgana*, who appears as a mirage over the Straits of Messina.

6 La Befana

This craggy old woman who declined an invitation to join the Three Kings bringing gifts to Christ in the manger regretted her decision, set out on her own, and has been travelling the earth with a sackful of gifts ever since. At Epiphany (6 January) she fills children's socks with presents if they've been good, or with coal (usually of the sweet, edible kind) if they've been bad.

7 Olive Oil

On 11 November, St Martin's Day, families celebrate their new, thick, spicy, green olive oil by sampling it on *i muffuletti*, round sandwich loaves baked with fennel seeds and dressed with salt and oil. If they don't have their own olive trees, families obtain a year's supply of olive oil from a relative or another trusted source, making sure to have a full *giara*, a waist-high terracotta storage jar.

8 Wine

A glass of new wine accompanies *i muffuletti* on St Martin's Day – usually strong, amber-coloured wine retrieved from the *botte* (barrel). Many families have at least enough grapevines for a yearly *botte* of wine, keeping it in the cellar if there is one and, if not, in the garage or anywhere else they can find as a cool spot.

9 Water Usage

Out of habit and necessity, Sicilians fiercely conserve water. Indoor plumbing did not reach the rural interior until the 1950s. Even where there is and has been plumbing, there is often no water due to poor piping and municipal mismanagement of local water supplies. Sicily is a land that, in theory, has plenty of water, but dry taps have been a frustrating problem for most areas since the mid-20th century.

Sicilian fisherman and his catch

10 Artisanal Fishing

Although fishing is big business, there are still artisanal fleets fishing Sicily's waters using *cannizzi*, handmade cane switches called fish-aggregating devices. Handmade lobster pots, and colourful nets are also used. Find artisans making *cannizzi* and pots and chat with fishermen who sell their own catch at local morning markets, or watch as they repair their nets later in the day.

Left **Giuseppe Tomasi di Lampedusa** Right **Luigi Pirandello**

🔟 Artists, Writers and Composers

1 Aeschylus

The "Father of Greek tragedy" (525–456 BC) was born near Athens but made extended visits to Sicily. Only seven of around 500 plays have survived the centuries, among them *Agamemnon*, *Oedipus* and *Prometheus Bound*. Many of his plays were premiered in Syracuse's theatre *(see p18)*, where they are still performed.

2 Antonello da Messina

Messina-born Antonello (c. 1430–79) is one of the masters of Italian Renaissance art, known for his exacting detail, intriguing portraits and the luminous quality of his paintings. He achieved the latter through his skilful use of oil paints, a technique he learned from Flemish masters. Italian Renaissance artists adopted oils in his wake and it became the standard medium for the world's greatest masterpieces. The few Antonello works that remain in Sicily are in museums in Palermo, Messina, Syracuse and Cefalù.

3 The Gagini Family

The Gagini family set the style for architecture and sculpture in Sicily during the 15th and 16th centuries. Inspired by elements of northern and central Italian art, the Gagini combined Renaissance and Gothic forms to create uniquely Sicilian pieces. Domenico (d.1492) was influenced by Ghiberti and Brunelleschi, and opened a workshop in Palermo. His son Antonello (1478–1536) produced delicately modelled, classic sculpture in the tradition of 15th-century Florence, in materials from marble to stucco.

4 Giacomo Serpotta

The Palermo-born artist (1656–1732) decorated Baroque interiors, creating an aesthetic transition between architecture and paintings by covering all available space with figures and scenes modelled in stucco.

5 Vincenzo Bellini

The composer (1801–35) was born in Catania, trained in Naples and is buried in Catania's cathedral. His successful early works led to commissions for La Scala in Milan. *The Sleepwalker* and *Norma* are among his most successful operas.

Antonello da Messina

Scene from *Norma* by Vincenzo Bellini

Luigi Pirandello
Born at Caos near Agrigento, Pirandello (1867–1936) is known as the founder of 20th-century drama. His best-known work is the play *Six Characters in Search of an Author* (1921).

Giuseppe Tomasi di Lampedusa
Lampedusa (1896–1957) is the author of *Il Gattopardo (The Leopard)*, the classic portrait of Sicilian aristocracy pre- and post-Unification. It was based on the life of his great-grandfather and published posthumously.

Salvatore Quasimodo
Born in Modica, Quasimodo (1901–68) wrote anti-Fascist works in a political climate that made it necessary to disguise his message. He was awarded the Nobel Prize in 1959.

Renato Guttuso
From Bagheria, Guttuso (1912–87) painted energetic canvases that spoke out against the Mafia and Fascism and illustrated Sicilian peasant life.

Leonardo Sciascia
Sciascia (1921–89) was a political essayist and novelist. Works such as *The Wine Dark Sea* give insight into the complicated world of Sicilian thinking and Mafia culture.

Top 10 Films Set in Sicily

1 La Terra Trema
Visconti's 1948 adaptation of Verga's *I Malavoglia*, the story of a fisherman's failed dream of independence.

2 Divorzio all'Italiana
Pietro Germi's 1961 comedy has Marcello Mastroianni as a Sicilian aristocrat seeking a divorce when divorce in Italy was not legal.

3 A Ciascuno il Suo
Adapted from a Sciascia novel, a look into the Mafia and life in 1960s Sicily, directed by Elio Petri in 1967.

4 Il Gattopardo
Luchino Visconti's 1968 film version of Lampedusa's novel stars Burt Lancaster.

5 Il Giorno della Civetta
A 1968 Mafia murder thriller adapted from Sciascia's novel *The Day of the Owl*.

6 Cento Giorni a Palermo
Giuseppe Ferrara's 1983 film documents the story of policeman Carlo Alberto Della Chiesa, murdered by the Mafia after just 100 days on the job.

7 Kaos
A 1984 film adaptation of four Pirandello stories.

8 Cinema Paradiso
Giuseppe Tornatore's 1989 Academy Award-winning film takes a romantic look at growing up in a remote village.

9 Il Postino
Shot on the island of Salina, this film is about a Sicilian postman whose life is turned around through his friendship with the Chilean poet Pablo Neruda (1994).

10 I Cento Passi
Marco Tullio Giordana recounts the life of anti-Mafia activist Peppino Impastato in this 2002 film.

Left **Teatro Massimo, Palermo** Right **Teatro Politeama Garibaldi, Palermo**

🔟 Performing Arts Venues

1 Teatro Antico di Segesta

At one of the most spectacularly sited theatres of the ancient world, experience Greek tragedy and comedy, modern dramatic productions, orchestral music with the Sicilian Symphonic Orchestra and the Orchestra of Teatro Massimo, plus world music from various guest artists. The theatre runs a full season with performances staged nightly from early July through to the end of August.
🔊 *Archaeological site • Map C3*

2 Greek Theatre, Syracuse

Classical works are staged during the spring in Syracuse's ancient theatre. Daily performances take place from mid-May through to the end of June. The largest, and one of the oldest, theatres of ancient Sicily is for the most part intact and accepts modern stage sets and seating. Don't miss one of Aeschylus's tragedies, which is held in the theatre where they premiered thousands of years ago *(see p18)*.

3 Archaeological Park, Selinunte

During the month of August performances of Greek drama, classical and modern dance, and music are staged among the ruins in Selinunte's archaeological park. Pick a spot among the temples and have a picnic under the stars. Performances start at 9pm *(see pp30–31)*.

4 Teatro Massimo & Teatro Politeama Garibaldi, Palermo

The Teatro Massimo was built in the 1880s as a symbol of post-Unification Sicily by Neo-Classical architects Giovanni Battista Basile and his son Ernesto. Although noted for its grandeur and superb acoustics, the theatre fell into decline and was closed for almost a quarter-century. After a massive renovation effort, the doors were reopened in 1997, and once again it is Palermo's premier venue for classical music, ballet and opera. Ballet as well as symphonic concerts can also be enjoyed at the city's Teatro Politeama, which roughly marks the border between old and modern Palermo *(see p88)*.

5 Teatro Massimo Bellini, Catania

Catania's great opera house, named after the much-loved local composer Vincenzo Bellini *(see p60)*, lies in the heart of the city. The grand theatre, influenced by the Paris Opéra, opened its doors

Teatro Massimo Bellini, Catania

For information on and tickets for performances at Syracuse's ancient theatre, visit www.indafondazione.org (tel. 0931 487 248).

in 1890 with a performance of Bellini's masterpiece *Norma* – the opera was so popular, Sicilians even named a pasta dish after it. The season of opera and concerts, including chamber music, and ballet performances by the theatre ballet company, runs from October through to June. ✆ *Via Perrotta 12, Catania • Map G4*

Luigi Pirandello statue, Teatro Luigi Pirandello

Lo Spasimo, Palermo

The open nave of Santa Maria dello Spasimo alla Kalsa, a former church, is a romantic venue for performances and film. Music can be heard from the upper outdoor terrace as well, while artworks are on display in the covered exhibition space. It is an innovative and resourceful use for one of Palermo's damaged historic buildings and one of the first venues to start the revival of the Kalsa neighbourhood *(see p88)*.

Teatro Luigi Pirandello, Agrigento

The ornate civic theatre of Agrigento was inaugurated in 1880 as the third-largest theatre in Sicily after the Teatro Massimo in Palermo and the Teatro Bellini in Catania. The venue was dedicated to the Agrigento native playwright Luigi Pirandello on the 10th anniversary of his death in 1946 *(see p61)*. The season runs from November through May with performances of modern theatre and dance, as well as, of course, productions of works by the great playwright himself, such as *Six Characters in Search of an Author*. ✆ *Piazza Luigi Pirandello 1, Agrigento • Map D4*

Il Piccolo Teatro dei Pupi e delle Figure, Syracuse

Puppeteers Mauceri and Vaccaro direct traditional puppet performances in the Catania style *(see p64)*, as well as plays of the lives of the saints, and the Mauceri family's own productions, such as *Alpheus*, based on the myth of Alpheus and Arethusa, and Euripides' *Alceste*. You can also watch puppets being made and antique puppets being restored in the family workshop down the street. ✆ *Via della Giudecca 17, Syracuse • Map H5*

Teatro Ditirammu, Palermo

This 52-seat theatre in Palermo's historic Kalsa district stages concerts of Sicilian folk music. It also promotes shows of lively tarantella or heart-wrenching storytelling set to music throughout the city – outdoors in Piazza Kalsa, for example. The theatre was founded by a family that has been involved with Sicilian music for generations, as illustrated in the museum next door. ✆ *Via Torremuzza 6, Palermo • Map P4 • www.teatroditirammu.it*

Opera dei Pupi di Enzo Mancuso, Palermo

The Mancuso family has been working with Sicilian puppets since 1928, and young Enzo dedicates himself to breathing new life into the art. He makes puppets as required, but his collection also includes vintage models handed down through the generations. ✆ *Via Collegio di Maria al Borgo Vecchio 17, Palermo • Map L1 • 091 814 6971 • www.mancusopupi.it*

Each November, Palermo hosts the Festival Morgana, which attracts puppeteers from around the world.

63

Left & Right **Puppets, Museo Internazionale delle Marionette Antonio Pasqualino, Palermo**

Puppet Traditions and Museums

Origins
There were puppeteers in ancient Syracuse, but the *opera dei pupi* as we know it today really became popular in the 1800s. Puppet theatres provided nightly entertainment for thousands of Sicilians – Palermo had more than 25 theatres where full houses would watch the good guys fight the bad guys in stories of adventure and romance, chivalry and treachery. Travelling puppet theatres drew huge crowds in smaller villages.

Catanese School
Puppets of the Catania tradition are almost 1.5 m (5 ft) tall. Puppeteers manoeuvre the heavy puppets via a metal pole attached to the heads, moving their limbs with strings. The puppets' joints are fixed and the swords of the paladins are constantly drawn. They inhabit a narrow stage with a long horizontal backdrop and are sometimes accompanied in the action by live actors.

Palermitan puppet

Palermitan School
Palermitan puppets are around 1 m (3 ft) tall. They are entirely manipulated by strings, have movable joints and can raise their face guards and draw their swords at will. Because they are lighter, they are more easily manipulated and their sword fights are much more lively. The stage of the Palermo-style theatre is a deeply recessed space with room for many characters and backed by elaborately decorated scenery.

Stories
The most traditional subjects are derived from the epic poems of the Carolingian cycle, retold by Ludovico Ariosto in his 1516 *Orlando Furioso*. Holy Roman Emperor Charlemagne and his paladins battle for Christianity against the Saracens and Turks, and raucous sword fights abound. Other productions relate the lives of the saints, stories of bandits, Shakespearean themes and local farces.

The Good Guys
Holy Roman Emperor Charlemagne and his paladins are dressed in armour and skirts and brightly coloured silks. Orlando, loyal leader of the paladins, carries a shield with a cross. His cousin Rinaldo, a brave fighter with a weakness for the ladies, is identified by the lion on his shield, as is his long-haired sister Bradamante, another warrior.

For places to see puppet theatre in action **See pp62–3**

Angelica, the object of the two men's affections, can be cunning but is usually on their side.

The Bad Guys
Mostly evil Saracens and Turks, they wear baggy trousers and droopy moustaches and bear shields decorated with a crescent moon. Charlemagne's brother-in-law and arch-enemy Gano di Magonza often tries to overthrow the crown. Sorcerer Malagigi plays both sides, sometimes helping, sometimes hurting the paladins' cause.

Museo Internazionale delle Marionette Antonio Pasqualino, Palermo
The extensive collection at this museum includes examples of puppet traditions from all over the world. Among the puppets, all of which are made by hand, and the stage equipment, are examples of famous Sicilian *pupari* (puppeteers) representing the Palermo and Catania schools, complete with puppets, stages and sets. A theatre puts on performances by Enzo Mancuso and his Compagnia Carlo Magno *(see pp63 and 86)*.

Museo Civico dell'Opera dei Pupi, Sortino
The collection is the patrimony of the Puglisi family, *pupari* for five generations. The master was Don Ignazio il Pastaro, who learned the craft from his father and passed it down to his sons and grandsons. He built up the collection of puppets, scenery and manuscripts by purchasing entire workshops of famous *pupari* from the areas around Catania and Syracuse as they went out of business. ✆ *Piazza S Francesco 9, Sortino • Map G5 • Call 333 892 11 82 for admission • Adm*

Assedio a Parigi
In this traditional story, Charlemagne, under siege by the Turks, sends Rinaldo to prepare the French army and Ruggero to Rome to ask assistance from the Pope. Ruggero spends the night at a castle, where he is served a poisonous dinner and dies. Rinaldo defeats a group of Saracens and then the Turkish leader himself. The sorcerer Malagigi predicts Rinaldo's and Orlando's duel over Angelica and convinces the cousins to end their differences and head to Paris to fight the Saracens. Orlando saves the day.

The Defeat of Roncisvalle and the Death of Orlando
In another famous tale, Charlemagne is tricked by his brother-in-law Gano and sends the paladins, led by Orlando, to accompany his bishop, who is to baptize a group of Saracens. But the paladins find themselves surrounded and outnumbered. After putting up a noble fight, Orlando dies on the battlefield.

Good guys Orlando and Rinaldo

Left **Via della Libertà, Palermo** Right **Sciacca ceramics**

🔟 Specialist Shops and Areas

1 Palermo and Catania

On and around Palermo's Via della Libertà and Catania's Via Etnea, you can shop in Italy's fashionable, classic stores for linens, clothing, shoes and handbags. Both boulevards offer a good mix of stores, boutiques and chic cafés.

2 Le Colonne, Taormina

Here you'll find elegant jewellery on Taormina's Corso. The proprietor makes each piece crafted to her own design, inspired by antique and historical motifs. Chunky necklaces of heavy gold with precious gems and rings set with antique incised stones are all unique items *(see p106)*.

The Corso, Taormina

3 Siculamente, Ragusa

Run by three young Sicilian entrepreneurs, here you can buy "T-scierts", caps, buttons and such with intriguing designs full of anti-Mafia symbolism and poignant sayings in Sicilian dialect. These include the fatalistic *Futtatinni* (nicely put, "Don't worry about it") or this romantic description of Sicily: *Unni l'aceddi ci vannu a cantari e li sireni ci fannu l'amuri* (Where the birds go to sing and the mermaids go to make love). ◈ *Via Carducci 50 • Map F5*

4 Punto Pizzo Free, L'Emporio, Palermo

An emporium in the heart of the city selling traditional products, books and crafts gathered from shops around Palermo whose owners have banded together refusing to pay the *pizzo* (the infamous Mafia protection money). There's safety in numbers, but these people are still on the front line, and their courage cannot be overstated. Buy a T-shirt, support the cause *(see p87)*!

5 Enoteca Picone, Palermo

To call Enoteca Picone a "wine bar" would hardly do it justice. Founded in the 1940s, it started life as a hole-in-the-wall that sold wine directly from the cask to the consumer, but now it is the place to go for its range of over 500 Sicilian, Italian and international wines. It's a popular meeting place for pre-dinner drinks, where you can sample your choice of wine accompanied by a platter of local meats and cheeses, surrounded by the serried ranks of bottles that line the walls. ◈ *Via Marconi 36 • Map J1*

Discover more at www.traveldk.com

6 De Simone Ceramiche d'Arte, Palermo

Brightly coloured ceramics with designs of jolly peasant farmers and fishermen going about their daily tasks *(see p87)*.

7 Ceramiche d'Arte F.lli Soldano, Sciacca

Alongside shops selling Sciacca's traditional green, yellow and blue ceramic dishes, the Soldano family produces traditional ceramics and modern designs on tableware and tiles. ✎ *Piazza Saverio Friscia 17 • Map C4*

8 Silva Ceramica, Caltagirone

In a courtyard off the piazza Silva Ceramica produces imitations of antique designs, including tiles. ✎ *Piazza Umberto I, 19 • Map F4*

9 Altieri 1882, Erice

Altieri produces ceramics in traditional styles as well as their own innovative designs. There are also pieces in gold, silver and coral in the decorative arts tradition of Trapani *(see p96)*.

10 Alessandra di Tommaso, Catania

This jeweller takes inspiration from archaeology and Baroque architecture, using semi-precious stones and lava in her exciting creations. ✎ *Via S Michele 11 • Map G4*

Siculamente, Ragusa

Top 10 Markets

1 Trapani
Each morning fishermen arrange their silvery catch along the wharf, yelling out its merits or holding it aloft for the benefit of prospective clients. ✎ *Map B2*

2 Selinunte
A lively 7am fish auction. Not to be missed. ✎ *Map B4*

3 Ballarò, Palermo
Palermo's most interesting market sells fish, produce and household goods. ✎ *Map L6*

4 Del Capo, Palermo
Step back into 19th-century Palermo in the streets of the Mandamento del Capo, crowded with farmers, housewives, butchers and every sort of meat imaginable. ✎ *Map J4*

5 Vuccaria, Palermo
One of Palermo's oldest markets – vendors really put on a show. ✎ *Map M4*

6 Syracuse, Ortygia
Rows of mussels, cherries, almonds, lemons – or whatever is in season. ✎ *Map H5*

7 Sciacca
Fishermen arrive in the afternoon, Monday to Friday, to sell their catch on the wharf. ✎ *Map C4*

8 Donnalucata
Each morning, under brightly striped awnings along the wharf, fishermen sell their catch. ✎ *Map F6*

9 Catania
Catania's market is famous for the variety of fish and the rowdy vendors. ✎ *Map G4*

10 Impromptu Markets
All over Sicily, farmers sell their own produce from the side of the road. You're likely to find wild asparagus, lemons, artichokes and cheese.

Left **Bar Duomo, Cefalù** Right **Piazza A Scandaliato, Sciacca**

🔟 Nights Out

1 Discos and Clubs

Discoteche open up each summer, often under new names and management. Huge crowds of visitors mix with locals who come from miles around to fill up the open-air dance floors and bars and the occasional billiard room. Look for posters for clubs, especially in towns and villages close to the sea.

2 The Piazza

In quiet villages, especially in summer when people stay inside during long, hot afternoons, families and friends get together in the piazza and eat *gelato* long into the night. In more touristy towns, the piazza assumes a pub atmosphere with live music and outdoor tables, such as the Caffè del Molo and Bar al Duomo at Cefalù.

Palermo nightlife

3 The Passeggiata

The *passeggiata* can be an afternoon or an evening activity. In summer, join the crowds on the promenades at Selinunte, San Vito lo Capo, Mondello, Marina di Ragusa, Palermo (Via Ruggero Settimo), Catania (Via Etnea) – or indeed anywhere a group might get together.

4 I Candelai, Palermo

This Palermo dive, which takes its name (as does the street) from the nearby former candle factory, has been going strong since 1996. Popular as a venue for live acts, arts events and tango lessons, it's a favourite with students from the nearby university. Membership is required for admission, but can be purchased at the door.
Ⓢ *Via dei Candelai 65 • Map K4*

5 Associazione Culturale Palab, Palermo

This lively cultural centre stages a wide range of events, from live music to comedy, theatre, dance, film and exhibitions of contemporary art and photography. There's a cocktail bar, pizzeria and restaurant, too *(see p88)*.

6 La Cuba, Palermo

In a spectacular setting among restored red domes and a gorgeous park, this is a popular eatery, bar and music venue with Palermo's bright young things. La Cuba also attracts its fair share of celebrities *(see p88)*.

For more on nightlife in Palermo **See p88**

Via Landolina, Catania

7 Via Landolina, near the Piazza Bellini, is lined with bars and clubs. Music is the main focus at the bar La Chiave (Nos. 64–70), which usually has a programme of live music and in summer organizes Landolina Live, a full slate of live rock, folk and jazz during June, July and August. ✆ Map G4

Agorà, Catania

8 A cool stream of water flowing through the rocks in the underground cave section of this lively bar and restaurant gives the place a unique atmosphere. The site has been in use from as far back as ancient Roman times, and now it lies below Catania's youth hostel (see p147), in the centre of town, beside the fish market. ✆ Piazza Currò 6 • Map G4

Zo, Catania

9 This dynamic arts and cultural centre is located on the premises of the same former sulphur works as Le Ciminiere (see p39). Performances of experimental music, dance and theatre are often staged here, as well as temporary exhibitions. Local talent is fostered, and there are also frequent inter-national partnerships. There is a café and restaurant, too. ✆ Piazzale Asia 6 • Map G4 • 095 746 3122 • www.zoculture.it

Lapis

10 This free publication has complete listings of music, theatre and art events. Separate editions are printed in Palermo and Catania, and they are a good way to find information about summer festivals. Pick up a copy at places in and around Catania, Palermo, Syracuse and Ragusa. ✆ www.lapis.it

Top 10 Features of the Passeggiata

1 **The Walk**
The key to the walk on the *passeggiata* is to do it *very* slowly.

2 **See**
Everybody checks out everybody else for everything from physical attributes, to fashion sense, to well-behaved children.

3 **Be Seen**
Wear the latest fashions, whether Dolce & Gabbana catwalk originals or market-stall copies.

4 **When and Where**
The prime time is Sunday afternoon or any day from dusk onwards. Walk around a piazza, down a *corso* or promenade, or anywhere people happen to gather.

5 **Who**
From babies in carriages to teens to grandparents, to entire families, couples and groups of friends, this is an open event.

6 **The Touch**
Everyone holds hands or entwines arms with their walking partners.

7 **Food**
The only things Italians consume while in motion are *gelato* or peanuts and the like.

8 **Men with Earpieces**
Pocket radios allow sports fans to stay abreast of the *partita* (football match) or Formula Uno motor racing.

9 **By Car**
Drive extremely slowly, with the windows rolled down so that you can chat.

10 **Spectator Sport**
Feel free to sit and watch the *passeggiata* go by, but sit side by side facing the action.

Left **Bread** Right *Gambero rosso*

Sicilian Dishes

1 Bread
Bread is a ritual in Sicily. Made from *grano duro* (semolina flour), once baked it is dense and golden, unlike any other bread in Italy. The shapes are particular to Sicily too, including braided loaves, and topped with sesame seeds. Bread is also used in main dishes – *mollica*, which are spiced and toasted breadcrumbs, often substitute cheese on top of pasta. Also look for *sfincione*, similar to a thick crust pizza eaten as a snack, and *focacce*, thin baked layers of dough filled with greens, sausage, ricotta or tomato.

2 Pasta
The amazing variety of pasta dishes makes use of all the bounty Sicily has to offer. A typical Palermitan dish is *pasta con le sarde* (with sardines, fennel, pine nuts, raisins and anchovies). The pasta itself, made with local durum wheat, is firm and full of flavour.

Maccheroncini con le sarde

3 Risotto
Rice dishes are as plentiful as pasta, and are particularly good with Sicilian lemons, *nero di seppia* (cuttlefish ink), greens or prawns. A real treat is the elaborate *Rippiddu Annivicatu*: rice is blackened with squid ink and shaped in a mound to resemble Mount Etna, a topping of ricotta cheese evokes the snowcap, and tomatoes the flames and lava flows.

4 Fish and Seafood
There is always an excellent choice of fish and seafood in Sicily. Look out for *sogliola* (sole), *triglie* (red mullet), *pesce spada* (swordfish), *tonno* (tuna), *mazzancolla* (large sweet prawns), *aragosta* (spiny lobster), *sarde* (sardines), *polpo* (octopus), *calamaro* (squid) and *gambero rosso* (red prawns).

5 Meat
Excellent lamb and pork are produced in Sicily. Sausages are always spiced and made with *semi di finocchio* (fennel seeds), stuffed in narrow casings and formed into continuous coils.

6 Caponata
Originally a fish dish, *caponata* was adapted by the *cucina povera* (kitchen of the poor) as a slow-cooked mix of aubergine (eggplant), tomato, celery, capers, olives, raisins and pine nuts, flavoured with vinegar and sugar, and topped with toasted almonds.

7 Arancini
A Sicilian fast-food treat, available in bars and from street vendors. Balls of rice are stuffed with a meaty tomato or vegetable *ragù* or ham and cheese, rolled in breadcrumbs, and fried. Their round, golden shapes resemble oranges *(arance)*, hence the name.

8 Panelle
Another snack food available from street vendors are these small squares of fried batter made from chickpea flour and a sprinkling of parsley, then topped with salt and lemon juice. They are often served in a sandwich.

9 Gelato
What makes Sicilian ice cream *(gelato)* so special is its base: a *crema* developed from Arab and Spanish culinary influences made with milk, or almond milk, and starch. It produces a rich, smooth and light dessert *(see p100)*.

10 Cassata and Cannoli
These classic Sicilian desserts are made with lightly sweetened ricotta. In *cassata*, ricotta and sponge cake are covered with marzipan and decorated with candied fruits. *Cannoli* are fried pastry shells filled with ricotta, candied fruit and chocolate chips.

Cassata

Local Produce

1 Cheese
Sicilian cheese comes from cows' or sheep's *(pecorino)* milk. Look for *primo sale*, aged *pecorino*, *tuma*, *caciocavallo* and *Ragusano*.

2 Ricotta
A cheese by-product used for sweet and savoury dishes. Available fresh, baked, or salted and aged *(ricotta salata)*.

3 Capers
From tiny buds to the huge *cucunci*, the best come from Salina and Pantelleria.

4 Vegetables
Amazing bounty awaits at marketplaces and restaurants. Don't miss the long skinny *cucuzza* (squash) and spicy red garlic.

5 Citrus Fruits
Excellent lemons (there is a small, sweet variety) and oranges (with numerous blood-red varieties) abound.

6 Salt
Richly flavoured salt has been harvested from the sea near Trapani since Phoenician times *(see p94)*.

7 Durum Wheat
The secret behind Sicily's flavourful bread and pasta. The countryside is covered with wheat fields.

8 Almonds and Pistachios
Eastern Sicily is known for its production of these high-quality and richly flavoured nuts.

9 Tuna
You'll find this fish in every form: fresh, preserved in oil, and in a variety of cuts.

10 Olives and Olive Oil
Millions of olive trees produce excellent-quality table olives and thick, green aromatic olive oil.

Left **Barrels of Marsala wine** Right **Alcamo vineyards**

🔟 Wines and Wine Producers

1 Nero d'Avola
The classic Sicilian red, made from at least 80 per cent of grapes of the same name with added Perricone, is characterized by its intense ruby colour and flavour of aromatic herbs. It's produced over the entire eastern half of the island but the two largest producers are between Palermo and Cefalù: Regaleali and Duca di Salaparuta.

2 Bianco d'Alcamo
Eighty per cent Catarratto with a dash of Damaschino, Grecanico and Trebbiano make up this dry and fruity white. Abundant production (more grapes are grown in Trapani than any other Sicilian province) made this the classic Sicilian white. The area from San Vito Lo Capo to Castellammare and inland to Alcamo and Calatafimi is under DOC *(Denominazione di Origine Controllata)* protection.

3 Marsala
A fortified wine produced in Marsala since the 18th century *(see p92)*. Awarded a DOC in 1986, Marsala is produced as Fine, Superiore (aged at least two years), Riserva (aged at least four years) or Vergine and Soleras (aged at least 10 years). Made from Grillo, Catarratto and Inzolia grapes, the wine is amber with a rich perfume of citrus flowers and almonds.

Nero d'Avola wine label

4 Cerasuolo di Vittoria
The cherry-red, dry and fruity wine is made from a blend of Frappato, Calabrese and Nerello grapes grown near Vittoria in the province of Ragusa. Established producers are buying vineyards in the area to produce their own versions of Cerasuolo.

5 Malvasia and Passito
Producers on Salina leave their Malvasia delle Lipari grapes to dry out on the vine or on mats to concentrate the flavours to make a sweet, thick dessert wine. Pantelleria's Zibibbo grapes are treated in a similar way, left on the vine until the flavours have condensed to make a dessert wine with intense tastes of dried fruits and vanilla.

Marsala

6 Etna Bianco and Etna Rosso

Sicily's first DOC was awarded in 1968 to the southern and eastern zone of Mount Etna, where the white grapes Cataratto and Carricante flourish. Reds, mostly the Nerello Mascalese, grow around the volcano's base.

7 Regaleali

The estate near Valledolmo has been in the Tasca d'Almerita family since 1830. Alongside traditional Sicilian wines, Regaleali also bottles international varieties. Their reds, based on Nero d'Avola, include Regaleali Rosso and the Rosso del Conte; whites, primarily of Inzolia and their own Varietà Tasca, include Villa Tasca and Nozze d'Oro.

Graci red wine

8 Marco de Bartoli

Marco de Bartoli and his sons cultivate indigenous grapes and remain faithful to the traditions of their area. Their production includes classic Marsalas and the unfortified Vecchio Samperi, aged for 20 or 30 years.

9 Planeta

At his estate near Sambuca di Sicilia, Diego Planeta and family plant both indigenous and international grapes – taste La Segreta Rosso (Nero d'Avola with Merlot and Syrah).

10 Artisan Producers

Many artisan producers are making excellent wines. Look out for Fondo Antico, Occhipinti, COS, Graci, Frank Cornelissen, Palari, Girolamo Russo, La Moresca and Terra delle Sirene.

Top 10 Grape Varieties

1 Nero d'Avola
The powerhouse Sicilian red grape, cultivated in the eastern half of the island.

2 Frappato
Cultivated in the province of Ragusa, the primary grape of Cerasuolo di Vittoria.

3 Grillo
A white grape indigenous to western Sicily and the basis of Marsala and other whites.

4 Inzolia
Also called Ansonica, a white grape throughout western Sicily, used in Marsala and other wines.

5 Zibibbo
The grape of Pantelleria, used traditionally for the sweet *passito*, is now also popular for crisp white wines.

6 Nerello Mascalese
Primary red grape grown on the slopes of Mount Etna, blended with Nerello Cappuccio to make the deep, spicy Etna Rosso.

7 Malvasia di Lipari
Responsible for the fragrant wines of Salina, rich in flavours of almond and candied fruits.

8 Catarratto
A white grape all over the island, changing character depending on the micro-climate. Grown from Marsala to Alcamo, Salina and Etna.

9 Grecanico
White grape native to western Sicily and one of the primary components of Bianco d'Alcamo.

10 International Vines
Recent additions to Sicilian vineyards include Chardonnay, Cabernet Sauvignon, Merlot and Syrah.

Visits can be arranged to the Regaleali estate (tel. 0921 544 011) and Planeta (email: winetour@planeta.it).

Sicily's Top 10

Left Antica Dolceria Bonajuto, Modica Right Caffè Sicilia, Noto

🔟 Pasticcerie and Gelaterie

1 Caffè Sicilia, Noto

For more than a century, the Assenza family have been behind the counter and at work in the maze-like laboratory of the Caffè Sicilia. They hunt down the highest-quality ingredients in the region, working to preserve the Sicilian pastry-making tradition. They create pastries from the recipes of Noto's ex-monastery of Santa Chiara as well as from their own innovative recipes, such as chocolates with carob, chestnut or sweet basil filling, *giuggolena* (sesame seed, honey and orange zest bar) and herb-infused honey.
Ⓢ *Corso Vittorio Emanuele 125 • Map G5*

2 Verona & Bonvegna, Catania

Undoubtedly the best *pasticceria* and *gelateria* in Catania, and one of the very best in Sicily. You can watch the skilled pastry chefs at work, creating mouthwatering masterpieces such as little filled ricotta doughnuts and their famed *cannoli*, but it's takeaway only as there's no room for tables and chairs – and there may well be a queue. Ⓢ *Via Asiago 60 • Map G4*

3 Cistercian Monastery, Agrigento

The nuns at the monastery of the Santo Spirito still offer pastries from behind the grate. They may look like something you've seen at other shops, but take a bite and taste how special they are. Order ahead for the speciality, sweet couscous *(see p26)*.

4 Pasticceria Artigianale Grammatico Maria, Erice

Maria Grammatico spent many years in the orphanage inside Erice's cloistered San Carlo monastery, learning the nuns' centuries-old recipes for their *dolci*, the sale of which provided their keep. The sweets are the opposite of monastic life: colourful and luxurious – try *sospiri* (sighs), *cuori* (hearts) and *cuscinetti* (little pillows).
Ⓢ *Via Vittorio Emanuele 14 • Map B2*

5 Donna Elvira Dolceria, Modica

Elvira Roccasalva has a passion for traditional recipes, faithfully reproducing by hand the sweets formerly made by Modica's cloistered nuns. She also uses the best-quality ingredients from the region to create her own recipes: try the *carato*, made with carob flour, raisins and almonds. Ⓢ *Via Risorgimento 32 • Map G6*

Typical Sicilian *granita* ices

6 Antica Dolceria Bonajuto, Modica

Fig-filled *nucatoli* and citrus and honey *torrone* are displayed in this small, elegant shop. Their chocolate is still made using the ancient Aztec method of working the cocoa with sugar and spices. ⓈCorso Umberto I, 159 • Map G6

7 Gelateria Stancampiano, Palermo

This unassuming family-owned shop has the creamiest *gelato* in Sicily. The bow-tied staff proudly offer rows and rows of traditional and seasonal flavours served up in cones, cups and brioches. It's out of the city centre, but worth the walk. ⓈVia Aquileia 60 • Map N2

8 Pasticceria Cappello, Palermo

Two branches sell among the best pastries in Palermo. The *setteveli* cake, featuring seven different-flavoured chocolate layers, is an unmissable experience. ⓈVia Colonna Rotta 68 • Map J4 • Via Nicolo Garzilli 10 • Map K1

9 Pasticceria Russo, Santa Venerina, near Catania

Since 1880 the Russo family has been producing Catanese pastries using the finest of local ingredients, including pistachios, almonds, oranges and honey. ⓈVia Vittorio Emanuele 105 • Map G4

10 Pasticceria Arturo, Randazzo

This third-generation pastry shop specializes in sweets made with the local pistachios, plus Sicilian almonds and hazelnuts. Taste any of the rich and spicy pistachio pastries and excellent *granita* while sitting in the marble and brass interior or outside, enjoying the views of Randazzo. ⓈVia Umberto 73 • Map G3

Top 10 Desserts

1 Cassata
Layers of sponge cake and ricotta cream covered with colourful marzipan and candied fruits *(see p71)*.

2 Gelato
Try soft and creamy ice cream, *zabaglione*, *semifreddo* or the solid *pezzo duro*.

3 Granita
Gelato's older cousin, ice is added to flavourings such as jasmine, wild strawberry or almond.

4 Biancomangiare
A snow-white pudding from Arab and Spanish days made with almond milk or cow's milk and thickened with rice starch.

5 Cannolo
Ricotta cream in a fried pastry tube *(see p71)*.

6 Frutta di Martorana
Almond paste sculpted and painted to look like real fruit or other edibles.

7 Biscotti della Regina
Hard biscuits rolled in sesame seeds.

8 Cassateddi
Fried pockets filled with ricotta flavoured with chocolate, lemon or cinnamon, eaten at breakfast time.

9 Coseduce or Cuccidati
Traditional fig-filled biscuits that exist under various names in every part of the island. Elaborate versions are made for St Joseph's Day *(see p56)* and called *squartucciati*.

10 'Mpanatigghi
These Modican pastries imported by the Spanish Counts of Modica are *empanadas*, a pastry crust filled with chocolate, spices and ground beef.

Left **La Gazza Ladra** Right **Majore**

Restaurants

1 Ristorante Duomo, Ragusa Ibla

Chef Ciccio Sultano carefully selects each ingredient with which to prepare dishes faithful to Ragusan tradition, but with his own twist. In three small, bright, elegant dining rooms, every course is excellent, starting with the bread basket. Two different tasting menus let you try a bit of everything *(see p125)*.

2 Cin Cin, Palermo

Tucked away on a side street off Viale Libertà, and never out of favour with the locals, chef-owner Vincenzo Clemente's charming restaurant serves what he describes as "Sicilian Baroque" cooking, combined with the Cajun flavours of his Louisiana roots. Dishes may be simple or inventive, but are always superb. The half-day "market cooking" courses, culminating in the lunch that you've prepared, are always very popular with visitors *(see p89)*.

Typical Sicilian fish dish

3 La Madia, Licata

Combining seasonal local ingredients and flavours from his childhood with a passionate, creative philosophy, chef Pino Cuttaia's dishes dazzle the palate. The seven-course tasting menu is a culinary experience that merits the two Michelin stars he now holds. A cuttlefish "egg" served with squid ink couscous is a dish typical of the craftsmanship and inventiveness of this young chef *(see p115)*.

4 Ristorante Fidone Maria, Frigintini

Maria Fidone and her family can be found in the kitchen at their homely *trattoria*, preparing hearty Ragusan dinners. Everything is made in-house, including the pasta, bread, olive oil and liqueurs. For a first course, choose the thick broad-bean soup *(lolli)* or home-made pasta. For a second course, try stuffed chicken accompanied by stuffed aubergines (eggplants) *(see p125)*.

5 La Gazza Ladra, Modica

Chef Accursio Craparo and his staff offer a creative menu designed to help you appreciate the subtleties of Sicilian culture and history. Layers of flavours in almost mathematical preparations work together to present the diversity of Sicily on a plate. Sommelier Shingo Nagaj is at the ready with a suggestion as intriguing as your palate will allow. Dine in a minimal, stylish dining room in winter, and in a cozy, elegant garden setting in summer *(see p125)*.

Osteria Nero d'Avola, Taormina

Creative yet unimposing preparations of local fish come from the open kitchen. Look for game in season – Turi the chef is a hunter. He's known for his dedication to seasonal and local ingredients prepared well and without too many flourishes. The restaurant also stands out for its reasonable prices – not an easy thing to find in Taormina *(see p107)*.

La Cialoma, Marzamemi

In the great atmosphere of the piazza of Marzamemi, the ancient tuna fishery of Prince Villadorata's family, is La Cialoma. The name is a Sicilian term for the work songs sung by tuna fishermen of old. La Cialoma has a small menu and a big wine list. The food is fresh, simple and nicely prepared: try the excellent marinated sardines or, in season, the simple and delectable tuna braised with laurel *(see p125)*.

Majore, Chiaramonte Gulfi

It's worth the trek to Majore, perched on a hilltop with fine views over the Ragusa plains. Since 1896 this simple restaurant, in the back of a butcher's shop, has been serving the finest pork dishes you're ever likely to taste, including a vast range of salami *antipasti (see p125)*.

Pocho, San Vito lo Capo

You can't do better for a view than the terrace at Pocho, with Monte Cofano and the bay splayed out before you. Owner Marilù Terrasi is well-known for her couscous, and the wine list is made up of selected Sicilian labels *(see p97)*.

Cantina Siciliana, Trapani

Chef Pino Maggiore serves up Trapani's classic *kus kus al pesce* (fish couscous) in a quaint interior in the old Jewish ghetto. He also offers pasta dishes (including the sublime *pesto alla Trapanese*, with garlic, almonds, tomatoes and basil), mains and desserts (try the ricotta-filled *cassateddi*). The wine list is Sicilian *(see p97)*.

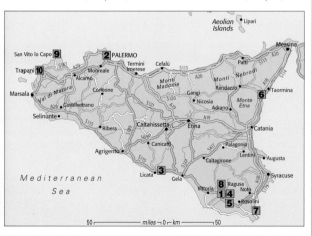

AROUND SICILY

SICILY'S TOP 10

Left **Museo Archeologico** Right **Palermo market stall**

Palermo

SETTLED BY THE PHOENICIANS IN THE 8TH CENTURY BC, *Palermo fell first to the Romans, then the Arabs, who chose Palermo for their capital, making the city one of the most magnificent and powerful in the world. This splendour was compounded during the Norman reign. Today what remains of earlier ages coexists with modern life: laundry billows off balconies of 15th-century palaces; buses rumble past even older buildings displaying a mix of east and west. Buildings destroyed in World War II have been left open to the sky, but Sicilians are ever resourceful: restaurants seat diners in crumbling, yet romantic courtyards, while a once-crumbling church is used as an arts venue.*

🔟 Sights

1. Norman Palermo
2. Quattro Canti
3. La Martorana & San Cataldo
4. San Domenico
5. Museo Archeologico
6. La Kalsa
7. Palazzo Abatellis
8. La Cala & Piazza Marina
9. Albergheria
10. The New City

La Martorana and San Cataldo

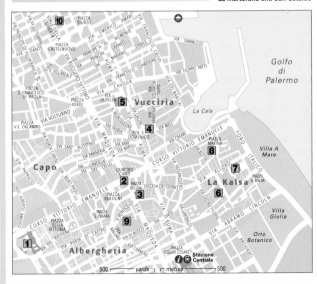

1 Norman Palermo

The splendid Norman kingdom in Sicily was marked by an exotic mix of cultures as manifested in their administration and in the architecture of the civic and private structures they commissioned *(see pp8–9)*.

2 Quattro Canti

The heart of town is marked by the intersection of Via Maqueda and Corso Vittorio Emanuele. Called the Quattro Canti (the four corners that divide Palermo into quadrants), each is swathed in sculptural decoration. The town hall is in the Piazza Pretoria just steps from the Quattro Canti, although the square is more commonly referred to as the Piazza della Vergogna (Square of Shame), after the shameless nudes perched around the edge of the elaborate fountain. Sculpted by the Tuscan Francesco Camilliani around 1555, the fountain was originally intended for a Florentine garden. ◈ *Map L5*

3 La Martorana and San Cataldo

In Piazza Bellini are two splendid churches. The little, mid-12th-century San Cataldo has three Arab-style, bulbous red domes in a row, latticed windows and an elegantly bare interior. But it is the Santa Maria dell'Ammiraglio next door that is the real gem. It was later renamed La Martorana after the Spanish patron who established a convent nearby. Notice the Norman bell tower (c.1140), now missing its red dome, and the 16th-century Baroque façade. Inside, ignore the later paintings in favour of the original mosaic decoration by skilled Byzantine craftsmen. Just inside the door, to the right, an image of King Roger, feet firmly on the ground, is shown being crowned by Christ, hovering in his ethereal realm *(see p44)*.
◈ *Piazza Bellini 3 • Map M5 • La Martorana: Open 8:30am–1pm, 3:30–5:30pm Mon–Sat, 8:45am–1pm Sun & hols • Adm • San Cataldo: Open 9:30am–1:30pm, 3:30–5:30pm Mon–Sat, 9:30am–1:30pm Sun & hols*

4 San Domenico Church, Oratorio del Rosario and the Vucciria

A warren of little streets northeast of the Quattro Canti is home to the Vucciria market *(see p67)*. Bordering the market to the north is the Church of San Domenico, burial place of notable Sicilians *(see p44)*. Rebuilt in the Baroque style in 1640, the harmonious yellow-and-white façade is 18th century. Behind the church is a Baroque chapel, the Oratorio del Rosario, with an altarpiece by Anthony Van Dyck.
◈ *Church of San Domenico: Piazza S Domenico; Map M3; Open 9am–12.30pm Mon–Sat ; Free;*
• Oratorio del Rosario: Via dei Bambinai; Map M3; Open 9am–1pm Mon–Sat; Adm

Oratorio del Rosario

The Mafia

During centuries of absentee sovereign power, Sicilians developed an inherent distrust of government, a fierce loyalty to their own (la cosa nostra), and learned to rely on justice administered by local bosses. After Unification in 1860, landowners employed thugs to intimidate and protect and the underworld system flourished. Using crime to create fear and form alliances, the Mafia soon infiltrated every crevice of society.

5 Museo Archeologico Regionale A. Salinas

Palermo's regional archaeology museum displays finds from sites all over western Sicily, from the Neolithic age through to the Roman period. Among Punic and Egyptian objects is the Palermo Stone (c.2700 BC), with a hieroglyphic inscription recording a delivery of 40 boatloads of Sicilian lumber to an Egyptian pharaoh. There are also numerous Etruscan artifacts, Greek vases and Greek and Roman sculpture, but the highlight of the collection are the Archaic and Classical metopes recovered from Selinunte (see pp30–33). ⊙ Piazza Olivella • Map L3 • Open 9am–1:15pm, 3–6:15pm Mon–Fri; 9am–1:15pm Sat, Sun & hols • Adm

6 La Kalsa

The Arabs established their government in this area, and its narrow, winding streets later became a densely populated residential district. Sadly, it was heavily bombed during World War II, and although some of the buildings have been restored, their crumbling state seems to add to the atmosphere in this bustling part of the city. Highlights include the Baroque Chiesa Santa Teresa; the Santa Maria dello Spasimo church dating from 1506; the restored 1170 Norman church of La Magione, later the headquarters of the Teutonic knights; and the Catalan-Gothic Palazzo Aiutamicristo. Sicilians are ever resourceful and today many of the ruined buildings are being used inventively as restaurants and galleries. Stay alert if you're wandering this area at night, however. ⊙ Bordered by Foro Italico, via Lincoln, Garibaldi & Alloro • Map N5

7 Palazzo Abatellis

Sicily's regional fine arts museum is housed in the 15th-century palace of a Spanish official, deep in the La Kalsa neighbourhood. The permanent collection traces the development of the figurative tradition in Sicilian art, and the museum runs an active exhibition programme. Highlights include the door and courtyard of the building itself, a masterpiece of Gothic-Catalan architecture, the detached fresco of the Triumph of Death by an unknown 15th-century master, Antonello da Messina's Annunciation to the Virgin, and an enormous 14th-century Hispano-Moresque amphora (see p38). ⊙ Via Alloro 4 • Map P4 • Open 9am–6pm Tue–Fri, 9am–1pm Sat, Sun & hols • Adm

Triumph of Death fresco, Palazzo Abatellis

Yachts, Palermo port

8 La Cala & Piazza Marina

Yachts bobbing in the small port can be seen from the 15th-century church of Santa Maria della Catena, while palaces of Palermo's aristocracy line the Piazza Marina. In the centre of the lovely gardens is a statue of Garibaldi *(see p37)*. The 1582 Porta Felice leads out to the Foro Italico and the seafront, for good waterside walks. ◉ *Map N3*

9 Albergheria

Bordered by Corso Vittorio Emanuele and Via Maqueda, this rather run-down residential area is a maze of streets spanned with billowing laundry. The heart of the neighbourhood is given over to the Ballarò market *(see p67)*. Don't miss the 17th-century Chiesa del Carmine on Via Giovanni Grasso, with its stuccoed interior and frilly, polychrome cupola. ◉ *Map L6*

10 The New City

The wide, tree-lined boulevard Viale della Libertà travels west from the Teatro Politeama, where the sparkling modern city begins, full of shops and cafés. It passes the Giardino Inglese, laid out with palms, to Piazza Vittorio Veneto and Royal Park (La Favorita), once a royal hunting ground. ◉ *Map J1*

A Morning in La Kalsa and Albergheria

🕐 From Via Maqueda take the Piazza Santissimi Quaranta Martiri up to the Chiesa del Gesù for a look at the wild Baroque decoration of the interior. Beyond the church, enter the streets taken over by **Ballarò market** *(see p67)* and spend some time weaving your way through the overloaded stalls.

🍴 For a late breakfast, stop at one of the stalls serving *panelle (see p71)* or fried aubergine (eggplant) sandwiches.

From Piazza Ballarò, pass through the old neighbourhood and by the Church of the Carmine with its colourful dome and take the Via Case Nuove to Via Maqueda. Head into **La Kalsa** on Via Gorizia to Via Garibaldi 43, where you can still see parts of the magnificent original structure of the Palazzo Aiutamicristo. Continue down to Santa Maria dello Spasimo, where there may be contemporary art on view. Take the residential Via della Vetreria to Via Alloro and the regional fine arts museum in **Palazzo Abatellis** designed by Matteo Carnalivari.

Go south on Via Alloro until the Piazza d'Aragona and take a right into Via A Paternostro to the Piazza San Francesco. Have lunch at the **Antica Focacceria** *(see p89)*, sitting in the piazza under the Gothic façade of San Francesco, or in the marble and wrought-iron interior, where you can watch the chefs serving up Sicilian specialities. For dessert, there's always good *gelato* to be found in the shop in the piazza.

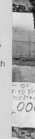

Around Sicily – Palermo

Following pages **Villa Palagonia, Bagheria (see p94)**

Left **Museo Internazionale delle Marionette Antonio Pasqualino** Right **Mondello**

Best of the Rest

1 Porta Nuova
This gateway to the city was erected in 1569 as a triumphal arch to commemorate Charles V's victory in Tunis. ◈ *Map J6*

2 Oratorio di Santa Zita
The interior of this chapel is covered with stucco decoration and Giacomo Serpotta's masterpiece of biblical and historical scenes (c. 1600). ◈ *Via Valverde 3 • Map M3 • 091 332 779 • Open Apr–Oct: 9am–6pm Mon–Fri, 9am–3pm Sat; Nov–Mar: 9am–3pm Mon–Sat • Adm*

3 Palazzo Mirto
One of the few surviving aristocratic *palazzi* in Palermo. The lavish interior is intact, with furnishings from the 18th and 19th centuries and allegorical frescoes. ◈ *Via Merlo 2 • Map N4 • Open 9am–7pm daily • Adm*

4 Castello della Zisa
From the Arabic *al-Aziz* (splendid), the palace lives up to its name, with stalactite ceilings, interior fountains, mosaic decoration and an ingenious ventilation system. The second floor houses a collection of Arab art. ◈ *Piazza Zisa 1 • Open 9am–7pm Tue–Sat, 9am–1pm Mon, Sun & hols • Adm*

5 Palazzo Belmonte Riso
In this 18th-century palace, the Museum of Modern and Contemporary Art exhibits international as well as Sicilian artists. ◈ *Corso Vittorio Emanuele 365 • Map L5 • Open 10am–7:30pm Tue–Sun • Adm*

6 Galleria d'Arte Moderna
A collection of contemporary international works in a splendid convent. ◈ *Piazza Sant'Anna • Map M5 • Open 9:30am–6:30pm Tue–Sun*

7 Museo Internazionale delle Marionette Antonio Pasqualino
An extensive collection of worldwide puppet traditions (see p65). ◈ *Piazzatta A Pasqualino 5 • Map P4 • Open 9am–1pm, 2:30–6:30pm Mon–Sat, 10am–1pm Sun • Adm*

8 Museo Pitrè
Founded in 1909, the museum displays folk art and furniture. ◈ *Viale Duca degli Abruzzi 1 • Map N1 • Open 9am–6pm Tue–Sun • Adm*

9 Cappuccini Catacombs
Burial site of Palermo's upper classes (1599–1881). ◈ *Via Cappucini • Open 9am–12:30pm, 3–5:30pm daily (closed Sun pm Nov–Mar) • Adm*

10 Mondello
This fishing village became a fashionable resort in the 19th century (see p50). ◈ *Map D2*

Castello della Zisa houses the Museo d'Arte Islamica.

Left **Via della Libertà** Right **De Simone ceramics**

TOP 10 Places to Shop

Via della Libertà
Upscale Italian chains line the boulevard between the Teatro Politeama and Piazza Crispi: try Frette (No. 36) for linens, Furla (No. 14) for leather goods, Michael Kors (No. 35) for luxury accessories and Max Mara (No. 16/a) for women's fashions. ◎ *Map J1*

Via Enrico Parisi
For menswear, step just off Via della Libertà to find high fashion at Uomo Store (No. 21/c) and chic boutiques such as Visiona Uomo (Nos. 11–13). Afterwards, stop in at the equally chic Il Baretto, round the corner in Via XX Settembre 43, for an *aperitivo*. ◎ *Map J1*

De Simone
The de Simone family has been producing high-quality hand-painted ceramics for generations, with designs illustrating jolly Sicilian farmers and fishermen. ◎ *Via Cavour 38 • Map L3*

Vincenzo Argento
For four generations the Argento family has been practising the art of puppetry. They make traditional puppets in the Palermitan style for sale and for use in their nearby theatre. ◎ *Via Vittorio Emanuele 445 • Map L5*

Rinascente
Italy's most upmarket department store has an outlet on this busy shopping street. There's a good selection of Italian *haute couture* and accessories, and a particularly good houseware department. ◎ *Via Roma 289 • Map M4*

Franco Bertolino
Hand-painted *carrettini*, traditional Sicilian miniature carts, are sold here along with beautifully crafted papier-mâché figures and fruit. ◎ *Salita Artale 8, corner Piazza Settangeli • Map K5*

Enoteca Picone
As well as over 7,000 different wines, liquors and beer, you'll find olive oil, cheeses and goodies for a special *aperitivo* (see p66).

Punto Pizzo Free, L'Emporio
The traditional products sold here come from various boutiques around the city, the owners of which have courageously refused to pay the *pizzo*, or Mafia protection money (see p66). ◎ *Corso Vittorio Emanuele 172 • Map M4*

La Coppola Storta
The traditional Sicilian cap has been given a new lease of life thanks to this innovative store. All sorts of creative versions of the hat are available. ◎ *Via Bara all'Olivella 74 • Map L3*

Markets
Some of the best shopping in Palermo happens at the three daily food markets. They are well worth visiting even if you don't intend to buy anything (see p67).

For tips on shopping in Sicily See p133

Left **Teatro Massimo** Right **Outdoor bar, Piazza Olivella**

Nights Out

Teatro Massimo
Palermo's historic theatre opened in 1897, then went into decline, but it was reopened in 1997 after a major restoration effort. It stages lyrical opera, ballet and symphonic concerts. *Piazza Verdi • Map K3 • www.teatromassimo.it • Guided tours*

Teatro di Verdura
A summer season of opera, ballet, concerts and plays is presented in this outdoor theatre in the garden of the former villa of the Prince of Castelnuovo. *Viale del Fante 70/b • Map N1*

Teatro Politeama Garibaldi
This Neo-Classical theatre was opened in 1874. The season offers symphonic concerts and ballet. *Piazza Ruggero Settimo • Map K2 • 091 607 2511/2532*

Teatro Biondo Stabile
Founded by the Biondo brothers in 1903 as a centre for experimental theatre, it is still fulfilling its mission. *Via Teatro Biondo 11 • Map L4 • 091 743 4300*

Santa Maria dello Spasimo
Lo Spasimo is a bombed-out church that acts as an amazing venue for an art gallery and a full programme of films and concerts (classical, contemporary, jazz), romantically staged in the roofless nave and garden space out the back. *Via dello Spasimo 15 • Map P5 • 091 616 64 80 • Open 9:30am–5:30pm daily • Free*

Associazione Culturale Palab
A combination of cultural centre, theatre, music and comedy club, cinema, cocktail bar, pizzeria and restaurant, this place is always buzzing with activity. *Piazza del Fondaco (Piazza Vittoria) • Map K3 • 091 651 55 27 • www.palab.it*

Via dei Chiavettieri
This pedestrian street buzzes with life well into the early hours of the morning. It is lined with clubs and pubs, many of which have outside tables and live music. *Map M4*

Teatro Co-Op Agricantus
Agricantus is a performing arts co-op staging high-quality theatre and music, particularly for children. *Via XX Settembre 82 • Map J1 • 091 309 636 • www.agricantus.org*

Piazza Olivella
At night the piazza between Teatro Massimo and Via Cavour fills up with university students hanging out in the many bars lining the square. *Map L3*

La Cuba
This multipurpose venue in the beautiful Villa Sperlinga, a little way out of central Palermo, draws a smart crowd with good food, drinks and music. Events are often held here *(see p68)*. *Villa Sperlinga, Viale Francesco Scaduto • Map N2 • 091 309 201*

Pick up a free copy of Lapis (see p69) for listings of all music, theatre and art events in and around Palermo.

Price Categories

For a three-course meal for one with half a bottle of wine (or equivalent meal), taxes and extra charges.

€	under €25
€€	€25–€35
€€€	€35–€55
€€€€	€55–€70
€€€€€	over €70

Above **Antica Focacceria**

TOP 10 Places to Eat

1 Cin Cin
Italian-American Vincenzo melds traditional Sicilian with a touch of the bayou. Creative cuisine and a warm welcome (see p76). ✆ Via Marin 22 • Map P2 • 091 612 40 95 • Closed Sun • €€€

2 Piccolo Napoli
Try the pasta with lobster or any fish dish at this family-run *trattoria* in the little market square behind the Teatro Politeama Garibaldi. ✆ Piazzetta Mulino a Vento 4 • Map K2 • 091 320 431 • Closed Sun • €€€

3 Osteria Mercede
Near Teatro Massimo, this small place serves delectable fish dishes that marry tradition and innovation. The chalkboard menu changes daily according to the catch. ✆ Via Pignatelli Aragona 52 • Map K3 • 091 332 243 • Closed Sat & Sun L • €

4 Lilla e Totuccio
This street-food eatery frequented by young *Palermitani* offers simple, tasty food, including pasta dishes. Even with wine, it's a bargain. ✆ Via Bara all'Olivella 91 • Map L3 • 320 292 62 55 • No credit cards • €

5 Antica Focacceria
Palermitan fast food and main courses under the façade of San Francesco. Sandwiches, *panelle* (see p71), focaccia and pasta. ✆ Via A Paternostro 58 (Piazza S Francesco) • Map M4 • 091 320 264 • €€

6 Ferro di Cavallo
Join the locals at this casual *trattoria* not far from the Quattro Canti for traditional fare and great people-watching. ✆ Via Venezia 20 • Map L4 • 091 331 835 • Closed Sun • €

7 Freschette
An organic, vegetarian café and market featuring local produce. ✆ Piazzetta Monteleone 5 • Map L3 • 091 982 07 27 • Closed Mon • €€

8 Zia Pina
Brusque service and shabby decor, but arguably the best seafood in town, and at a bargain price. ✆ Via Argenteria 67 • Map M4 • 331 981 45 46 • Closed dinner • €

9 Osteria dei Vespri
A chic spot in a *palazzo* used in Visconti's film The Leopard. ✆ Piazza Croce dei Vespri 6 • Map M5 • 091 617 16 31 • Closed Sun • €€€

10 Bye Bye Blues
Excellent Sicilian ingredients are chosen for inventive dishes. ✆ Via del Garofolo 23, Mondello • Map D2 • 091 684 14 15 • Closed Tue • €€€

Note: Unless otherwise stated, all restaurants accept credit cards and serve vegetarian meals.

Left **Selinunte** Right **Trapani** harbour

Northwest Sicily

F AR FROM THE DEVELOPED RESORTS OF THE EAST COAST, *much of this area was remote until relatively recently and presents unique opportunities to wander through fishing villages, watch shepherds at work and witness a way life that has survived for centuries. The coastal areas and offshore islands are pristine, while the mountainous interior, part rocky, part arable, has some of the harshest terrain in Sicily – water is scarce, the heat relentless and earthquakes are not infrequent. The villages of the interior lost large percentages of their population to mass emigration over the last century (see p37) but those who remain are largely small farmers still using mules to work their fields, or younger generations turning their talents towards developing vineyards of local grapes to produce high-quality Sicilian wines.*

🔟 Sights

1	Monreale	**6**	Pantelleria
2	Selinunte	**7**	Marsala
3	Trapani	**8**	Motya
4	Segesta	**9**	Egadi Islands
5	Lo Zingaro	**10**	Erice

Marsala

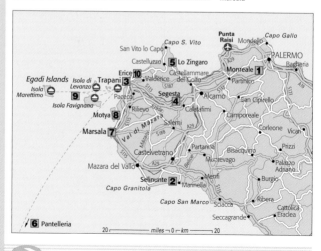

Cloister, Monreale

Monreale

On this royal hill *(mons reale)* Sicily's Norman king, William II, built the mosaic-encrusted monastery and cathedral that proved to be the last and most splendid of the island's Norman monuments *(see pp10–11)*.

Selinunte

The ruins of this Greek city, including temples, walls, market-place and homes, stand majestically backed by the sea – silent reminders of the glory of the once great city *(see pp30–33)*.

Trapani

A busy port since the Phoenicians landed here, it gained importance during Spanish domination as the closest port to Spain, and it's still a bustling area. The modern town has ballooned, but the quaint and lively historic centre is concentrated on the tiny sickle-shaped peninsula – the entire area covers less than 2.5 sq km (1 sq mile). The perpendicular main streets are lined with a mix of Baroque buildings, shops and cafés. Via Torrearsa leads from the port to the market square with its lovely loggia. The Corso leads to the tip of the peninsula, with glimpses of everyday Sicilian life in the side streets. ◈ *Map B2*

Segesta

The most romantic ruins in Sicily are tucked between the green hills and rugged mountains just west of Calatafimi. The temple was built in perfect, solid Doric proportions (c.420 BC) and stands isolated on a gentle slope, turning a beautiful shade of pink in the sunset. The un-grooved columns, missing *cella*, and still-attached studs around the *stylobate* hint that it was left unfinished. The theatre, high up on Monte Barbaro, has views to Castellammare del Golfo *(see p50)* and is still in use *(see p62)*.
◈ *4 km (2 miles) from Calatafimi*
• *Map C3* • *Open Apr–Oct: 9am–7pm, Nov–Mar: 9am–4pm* • *Adm*

Lo Zingaro

Sicily's first nature reserve was instituted in 1980 to protect 7 km (4 miles) of rocky coastline on the Tyrrhenian Sea between Scopello and San Vito lo Capo. Marked trails of various levels of difficulty traverse the steep interior, or creep along the cliff above the sea, occasionally forking down to small coves with pebble beaches. The reserve protects flora and fauna such as wild orchids, limonium, wild carnations, dwarf palms, iris, remains of once widespread ilex and cork-oak forests, lichens and ferns, Bonelli's eagles, Peregrine falcons, Sicilian warblers, owls, porcupines and foxes. ◈ *Map B2*

Segesta

Marsala Wine

Marsala was "discovered" by John Woodhouse in the 18th century when he shipped some local wine to Liverpool, conserving it with added alcohol. The business took off, with Woodhouse, plus Englishmen Ingham and Whitaker and the Italian Florio, fortifying wine purchased from peasant farmers. During the 20th century industrial versions gave it a reputation as a cooking wine, but since the 1970s producers have been working to produce high-quality Marsala once again.

Pantelleria

This tiny volcanic island, closer to Africa than Italy, is as well-known for its VIP visitors as for its natural beauty and culinary gifts. The architecture reflects Arabic influences and the island is dotted with *dammusi* – low, whitewashed, domed houses. Pantelleria is renowned for its top-quality caper production and the thick and sweet *passito* wine, made from the native Zibibbo grape, which grows well despite the ever-present *scirocco* winds that blow from the sea. ◈ *Map A6 • Hydrofoils: Ustica Lines 0923 911 502 • Flights: Palermo and Trapani*

Pantelleria

Marsala

This sunbaked seaside town was founded in 397 BC as Lilybeo by Carthaginians fleeing Motya. It finally fell to the Romans after a 10-year siege, but it was the Arabs who named the city: Marsa Allah, meaning "the port of God". Today, the town is best known as the landing point for Garibaldi's Redshirts *(see p37)* and for the wine that borrowed its name. The city survived successive invasions, but came into its own in the 18th century, when the Marsala wine trade was born. The Baglio Anselmi is an archaeological museum that houses the treasures of Marsala's Punic past, including the relics of a huge warship, excavated in 1971 and dating from around 240 BC. ◈ *Map B3 • Museo Archeologico Baglio Anselmi: Lungomare Boéo; Open 9am–7pm Tue–Sat, 9am–1pm Sun & hols; Adm*

Motya

This archaeological park occupies an entire island in Lo Stagnone, the lagoon north of Marsala, where the 8th-century BC Phoenician and later Carthaginian city thrived. Dionysus I of Syracuse destroyed Motya (Mozia in Italian) in 398 BC, leaving ruins of intricate fortifications, docks, homes decorated with mosaic flooring, and other structures. The extensive archaeological collections of the Museo Whitaker (former home of the English Marsala-producing family) are displayed as Whitaker intended – the highlight is the outstanding Greek marble statue of a youth in a diaphanous pleated tunic (c.440 BC). ◈ *Map B3 • Museo Whitaker: Open 9am–1pm, 2:30–6pm daily; Adm*

Salt fields, Motya

9 Egadi Islands

Levanzo, Favignana and Marettimo can be reached from Trapani in as little as 20 minutes by hydrofoil and are great for relaxing on a summer's day, as there is pretty much nothing here except for the sea. They are most famous for the *mattanza*, the Arabic tuna-fishing ritual that is still practised here in spring. Favignana is dotted with tufa quarries that give the island a pockmarked look; the caves of Levanzo's interior have Paleolithic and Neolithic paintings, and the swimming is good on all three islands. Marettimo, the furthest from the mainland (1 hour from Trapani), is known for its extraordinarily clear waters. ◈ *Map A3*
• Hydrofoil and ferry: Trapani

10 Erice

On top of a cliff above Trapani, ancient Eryx was known for its temple to Venus Erycina so large that it served as a beacon to sailors at sea. The temple was replaced with a castle in the Middle Ages, and the village, renovated at the same time, still has a medieval appearance. The main industry here is tourism, but it's a nice visit: local artisans make good ceramics and rugs, and the views are spectacular – on a clear day you can see all the way to Africa. ◈ *Map B2*
• www.funiviaerice.it

A Day Exploring Trapani

Morning

🕐 Start the day with a visit to Trapani's colourful market, which is held at the port, at Torre de Ligny. Well-stocked vendors are happy to offer tastes of cheeses, olives and tuna to potential customers. This is a great place to pick out a few things for a picnic, or you can visit Il Tonno in Piazza, in Piazza Mercato del Pesce, for a range of typical Sicilian delicacies. Next, walk up Corso Vittorio Emanuele and take a look at **Perrone Ceramiche Souvenir**'s hand-crafted ceramic pieces *(see p96)*.

When Corso Vittorio Emanuele runs into Via Torrearsa, walk a few hundred metres to the right to visit the church of Sant'Agostino, with its 14th-century rose window, before passing through the arch and back onto Via Torrearsa. Going down Corso Vittorio Emanuele, crane your neck to see the green majolica domes of San Lorenzo Cathedral, before reaching the end of the peninsula to enjoy your lunch and the sea views.

Afternoon

If you haven't spent all day shopping in Trapani, spend the afternoon up in **Erice**, with its good picnic sites and superb views. Or take the hydrofoil to the **Egadi Island** of Favignana.

Make it back to Trapani in time for the sunset to take part in the local *passeggiata*, then enjoy a wonderful fish dinner at **Taverna Paradiso** *(see p97)*.

Left **Castelvetrano** Right **Baroque palace, Bagheria**

Best of the Rest

1 Ossario di Pianto Romana
With sweeping views to the Golfo di Castellammare and Erice, an obelisk commemorates Garibaldi's defeat of Bourbon forces in May 1860 *(see p37)*. The victory allowed him to take Palermo, then all of Sicily, and eventually led to the Unification of Italy. ✎ *Map C2*

2 Castelvetrano
The "City of Olives and Temples", known for its olive oil production, can thank the Arabs for its urban plan and its central maze of piazzas. The bronze *Ephebus* (c.470 BC) is the pride of the Museo Civico. ✎ *Map B3*

3 Mazara del Vallo
This fishing port is home to the lovely Hellenic bronze statue of the *Satiro Danzante* ("dancing satyr"), found on the seabed by fishermen in 1997. ✎ *Map B3*

4 Bagheria
This village east of Palermo is now rather built up, but you can still see the elaborate Baroque villas built by Palermo's nobility, when it was all citrus groves and orchards. ✎ *Map D2*

5 Cusa Quarries
This natural quarry for Selinunte is located amid olive trees, with blocks of tufa and partially extracted columns. Slaves would have hauled columns 9 km (6 miles) to Selinunte.
✎ *Near Campobello di Mazara • Map B3*

6 Alcamo
This small village has a 14th-century castle of the Spanish Counts of Modica, who once ruled much of the region. It is best known for Bianco d'Alcamo, a white wine with DOC protection. ✎ *Map C2*

7 Marinella di Selinunte
The fishing village at Selinunte has a great morning market and a historic centre of fishermen's homes around the small port. The boardwalk is lined with bathing establishments, restaurants and bars. ✎ *Map C4*

8 Solunto
The Greek village of Solus was built on top of a Carthaginian settlement, high above the sea. Lacking natural springs, it had a highly developed water conservation method. Among the ruins are cisterns, channels and pools. ✎ *Map D2*

9 San Vito lo Capo
On this dramatic promontory on the northwestern tip of Sicily is a resort with a long sandy beach and a promenade action-packed in summer. ✎ *Map B2*

10 Saline, Saltpans
Exceptional sea salt is produced here using 16th-century windmills. The Museo del Sale in Paceco explains production *(see p54)*. ✎ *Map B2*
• *Museo del Sale: Via Chiusa, Nubia Paceco; Open 9:30am–7pm daily; Adm*

Both parents of American baseball legend Joe DiMaggio emigrated to the USA from the Isola delle Femmine.

Left **Belice Valley** Right **Castellammare beach**

🔟 Landscape Features

1 Rolling Hillsides
The rolling hills of the Belice valley are planted with wheat – green in winter, gold in summer, and burned black after the harvest – bordered by grape vines and olive trees. 🗺 *Map C3*

2 Poggioreale Hill
On the road from old to new Poggioreale, a single wheat-covered hill rises up, topped with a lone wild pear tree. 🗺 *Map C3*

3 Rugged Mountains
The rugged hills around Segesta, Calatafimi and Alcamo look dry and barren, but resourceful Sicilians plant them with hearty vines, cultivating the hills as high as possible. 🗺 *Map C3*

4 Quarries
The rocky mountains between Trapani, Castellamare del Golfo and San Vito lo Capo are rich in marble, but are slowly being destroyed by huge industrial quarries extracting the stone for office buildings. 🗺 *Map B2*

5 Faraglione
The rock towers at Scopello Tonnara jut out of the water, and are circled by seagulls who nest in the rocks' crevices. 🗺 *Map C2*

6 Promontories
The enormous rocky formations hurled up by the sea include Monte San Giuliano (with Erice on top), Monte Cofano (with spectacular bays and a great view from Erice), and Monte Monaco at San Vito lo Capo. 🗺 *Map B2*

7 Belice Valley
Near its mouth the wide, fertile Belice Valley is long, low, flat, and very good for farming; it's covered with a patchwork quilt of wine vineyards, olive groves, melon vines and citrus fruit trees. It is traversed by a typical Sicilian highway, raised on tall stilts.

8 Erosion
The Romans deforested Sicily to make way for profitable wheat farms. The result here is treeless earth, parched for much of the year and prone to drastic run-off during rains. When flooded with more water than they can handle, entire hillsides crumble into the sea.

9 Beaches
Long sandy beaches line the western coast of Sicily, reaching up to the huge stretch of sand at San Vito lo Capo. Pebble beaches are found to the northwest, on the coast of the Golfo di Castellammare.

10 Plain
The mountains of the interior flatten as they near the sea toward Mazara, Marsala and up to Trapani on the northwest coast. The flat, sunbaked ground is fertile territory for grapes, olives and the saltpans.

Left **Cantine Florio** Right **Cantine Pellegrino**

Traditional Shops

1 Pasticceria Artigianale Grammatico Maria, Erice
This specialist sweet shop offers a wide range of delicious treats made according to recipes that have been collected over the centuries by the sisters of Erice's San Carlo monastery *(see p74)*.

2 Perrone Ceramiche Souvenir, Trapani
In addition to ceramic plates, this family business produces traditional figurines of Sicilian peasants for nativity scenes and miniature terracotta replicas of traditional foods. ❧ *Corso Vittorio Emanuele 106 • Map B2*

3 La Casa del Tonno, Favignana
The name, the House of Tuna, says it all. In central Favignana, site of the *mattanza (see p42)*, shop for canned tuna in oil and *bottarga* (dried tuna egg). ❧ *Via Roma 12 • Map A3 • www.iltonno.it*

4 Altieri 1882, Erice
Since 1882 Altieri has been producing their own uniquely designed pieces in gold, coral and ceramics. ❧ *Via Cordici 14 • Map B2*

5 Cantine Florio, Marsala
Inside the Florio institution is a nice store and a wine museum with a selection of antique tools used for winemaking. ❧ *Via Vincenzo Florio 1 • Map B3 • www.duca.it/cantineflorio*

6 Cantine Pellegrino, Marsala
This established Marsala family offers tours (in various languages) of the cellars and tastings. ❧ *Via del Fante 39 • Map B3 • www. carlopellegrino.it*

7 Gustibus, Trapani
A great selection of wines, liqueurs, oils, honey and handmade local products such as ceramics and coral and lava jewellery. ❧ *Corso Garibaldi 119 • Map C2*

8 La Bottega del Pane Rizzo, Castelvetrano
Master baker Tommaso Rizzo uses local ingredients, natural yeast and a wood-burning oven to make the traditional *pane nero di Castelvetrano*, a tasty dark-brown bread. There are also the delicious *biscotti piccanti*, biscuits made with black pepper and anise. ❧ *Via Garibaldi 85 • Map B3*

9 A Maidda, San Vito lo Capo
A nice selection of Sicilian treats and wines – but they don't come cheap. ❧ *Via Savoia 87 • Map B2*

10 Museo del Sale, Trapani
The museum store sells boxes of traditionally produced sea salt. Sea salt's rich flavour can vary, along with its saltiness, according to climatic conditions; the fine grain of the stone-ground salt adds texture to foods *(see p94)*.

Note: Cantine Florio and Cantine Pellegrino are open only by appointment. See their websites for details.

Price Categories

For a three-course meal for one with half a bottle of wine (or equivalent meal), taxes and extra charges.

€	under €25
€€	€25–€35
€€€	€35–€55
€€€€	€55–€70
€€€€€	over €70

Above **Buffet of traditional fare at Agriturismo Vultaggio**

🔟 Places to Eat

1 Taverna Paradiso, Trapani
Locally caught fish prepared simply and with great skill is on the menu here. Welcoming interior, congenial service and a good wine list. ⊗ *Lungomare Dante Alighieri 22 • Map B2 • 0923 22 303 • Closed Sun • €€€*

2 Pocho, San Vito lo Capo
Dine in an eclectic dining room with puppets hanging in the corners or on the breezy terrace looking down at Monte Cofano and the bay (see p77). ⊗ *Località Isulidda, Makari • Map B2 • 0923 972 525 • Closed Oct–Easter • €€€*

3 Cantina Siciliana, Trapani
Pino Maggiore's restaurant, in Trapani's historic ghetto, offers excellent traditional fare, such as couscous and Trapani's almond pesto (see p77). ⊗ *Via Giudecca 32 • Map B2 • 0923 28 673 • €€€*

4 Ristorante La Terrazza, Scopello
Enjoy fresh fish, caught for the restaurant by a local fisherman, and the views of Scopello's Norman and Aragonese watch-towers. ⊗ *Via Marco Polo 5 • Map C2 • 0924 541 198 • Closed Tue (mid-Sep–mid-Jun), Jan–Feb • €€€*

5 La Bettola, Favignana
There is no menu here; just the catch of the day and a few vegetable dishes. A good place in spring, when the tuna are running. ⊗ *Via Nicotera 47 • Map A3 • 0923 921 988 • Closed Thu, mid-Nov–Jan • €€*

6 Le 4 Stagioni, Menfi
At this hotel restaurant and pizzeria the watchword is quality, whether it be for sea-fresh fish, pasta dishes or pizzas. There is a wonderful view over the sea from the terrace. ⊗ *Via delle Margherite15 • Map C4 • 0925 78447 • €€*

7 Agriturismo Vultaggio, Guarrato, near Trapani
Enjoy traditional Sicilian food at this agritourism farm that produces its own wine, oil and citrus fruits. The local Slow Food group holds events here. ⊗ *Contrada Misiliscemi 4 • Map B2 • 0923 864 261 • €€*

8 La Pineta, Selinunte
Expertly prepared fresh fish served on the beach under torchlight. ⊗ *Via Punta Cantone • Map B4 • 0924 46 820 • €€€*

9 Le Vele, Trapani
Le Vele is elegant but not over the top. As well as great pizzas, they serve fish cooked in traditional Trapani style, but their speciality is *patate alla vastasa*, spicy potatoes with onion and cheese. ⊗ *Via Serisso 18 • Map B2 • 0923 29 743 • Closed Mon • €*

10 Bricco & Bacco, Monreale
The fare is inspired by the hearty dishes of Sicily's rugged interior. Look for antipasti, meat (including *trippa*, or tripe) and a host of vegetable sides. ⊗ *Via Benedetto d'Acquisto 13 • Map C2 • 091 641 77 73 • Closed Mon (Jun–Aug: Sun) • €€€*

Note: Unless otherwise stated, all restaurants accept credit cards and serve vegetarian meals.

Left **Mount Etna** Right **Giardini Naxos**

Northeast Sicily

THE NORTHEAST OF SICILY CAN'T HELP BUT BE DOMINATED *by Mount Etna*, although the region also consists of three mountain ranges, a group of islands with another active volcano, and two of Sicily's largest cities. Parts of this area have been devastated by wars, earthquakes, tidal waves and lava flows, but the land and the people that live on it come back after each ordeal, heartier and more steadfast. Perhaps that is why people here celebrate feast days of their patron saints with so much fervour. High up in the hills and peaks of the Nebrodi and Madonie mountains, it often seems like nothing has changed for eons – the same castles that safeguarded the royal passageways of the interior now stand guard over modern *autostrada*.

🔟 Sights

1. Aeolian Islands
2. Taormina
3. Mount Etna
4. Cefalù
5. Catania
6. Giardini-Naxos
7. Messina
8. Straits of Messina
9. Madonie mountains
10. Tindari

Giardini Pubblici, Taormina

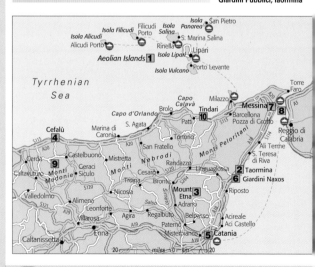

Aeolian Islands

1 The islands were declared a World Heritage Site by UNESCO in recognition of the ongoing evolution of the volcanic forms that creates their spectacular scenery. The islands remain an important study area for vulcanologists *(see pp12–13)*.

Taormina

2 Sicily's first true holiday resort has been drawing visitors for centuries, all of whom fall in love with its sparkling, colourful beauty *(see pp14–15)*.

Mount Etna

3 Europe's largest active volcano dominates Sicily – from much of the island it is rarely out of sight and never out of mind *(see pp16–17)*.

Cefalù

4 This small fishing village, now a resort thanks to its good sandy beaches, lies on a strip of and between the sea and a huge promontory looming above. Cefalù was founded in the 4th century BC, but destroyed by the Norman Count Roger in 1063. It only regained prominence thanks to his son Roger II, who endowed the village with a bishopric and a church decorated with exceptional Byzantine mosaics. The modern holiday

Cefalù waterfront

Duomo, Catania

resorts lie to either side of the town because the village itself has closed its doors to the sea, fortified itself against storms with tall protective stone walls, and focuses its attentions inwards *(see p101)*. ✪ *Map E2*

Catania

5 Sicily's second-largest city has had its unhappy share of earthquakes and volcanic eruptions and, although Catania is rich in monuments dating back to its Greek foundations, the city seen today was built mostly after the massive 1693 earthquake. The rebuilding was largely carried out in a unique Baroque style, utilizing the workable local black lava stone. The most important monuments are grouped around the Piazza Duomo with the 1736 Elephant Fountain, the Duomo itself, dedicated to Sant'Agata and retaining its original Norman apses, the Fish Market in Via Garibaldi *(see p67)*, the Roman theatre, the castle *(see p47)*, Via Crociferi with its Baroque palaces, and Via Etnea with its shops and cafés. ✪ *Map G4*

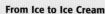

From Ice to Ice Cream

Greeks and Romans used Mount Etna's snowfall to chill their wine, and the Arabs, bringing with them sugar and citrus, used it to make cold, sweet drinks. Sicilian chefs were long accustomed to combining ice with sugar and natural flavours (lemon, jasmine, cinnamon) to make *granita* and sorbet, but by the beginning of the 1700s, whether they invented the concept or borrowed it from their mainland neighbours, they had perfected the craft of ice-cream-making, adding to their repertoire the chocolate brought by the Spanish from the New World. Sicilian *gelato* is now famous the world over *(see p71)*.

Giardini-Naxos
According to ancient historians Naxos was founded in 734 BC after a ship was blown off course as it sailed to southern Italy, and it became the first Greek settlement in Sicily. Naxos never became a powerhouse but was mother city to successive colonies and the setting off point for messengers carrying news back to Greece. The ruins, defensive walls and parts of a temple are enclosed within a nicely kept park. A small museum houses finds from the Greek site, as well as finds recovered from shipwrecks. ⓢ *Map H3 • Site and museum: Open 9am–7pm daily • Adm*

Messina
Founded by colonists from Messenia, Greece, the city grew up around the harbour, which has always been its focus. In 1908 Messina was levelled by a disastrous earthquake and tidal wave, although parts of the older city survive.

Monuments are concentrated around the magnificent harbour, including the Norman Duomo with original portals and sculpture, a 15th-century fountain in the Piazza Duomo and a clock tower whose mechanized figures come to life at noon with an elaborate lengthy display; the Santissima Annunziata dei Catalani with its Norman features, the 1572 monument to Don Giovanni of Austria; and the Museo Regionale, with works by Antonello da Messina *(see p60)* and Caravaggio. ⓢ *Map H2*

Straits of Messina
The narrow strait between Messina and Reggio di Calabria was supposedly guarded by Scylla and Charybdis, the mythical sea creatures who led sailors astray. A proposed suspension bridge linking Sicily and mainland Italy has been under debate for more than 30 years. Sicilians are split between those who believe a link to the mainland would open up Sicily to much-needed economic development, and those who fear a loss of their insularity, and thus autonomy. Many suggest that the island infrastructure should be addressed first – much of Sicily still lacks basic necessities such as decent roads and water and electricity supplies. ⓢ *Map H2*

View of Messina

Madonie mountains

Madonie Mountains

9 The Madonie range, featuring Sicily's highest peaks after Mount Etna, extends from Cefalù inland and is protected by the Parco Naturale Regionale delle Madonie. The park encompasses spectacular countryside, forests of beech, chestnuts, cork oaks, poplars and fir, and tiny villages that time seems to have forgotten. The remote villages that once provided refuge to bandits on the run are now good starting points for mountain hikes, horseback riding, cycling and skiing (see pp52–3). Map E3

Tindari

10 The extensive ruins of ancient Tyndaris, first Greek and then Roman, lie to either side of the Decumanus Maximus, the main street. Homes show mosaic flooring, drainage and the remains of heating systems. A restored basilica with graceful arches spans the street where it marked the entrance into the public areas. A theatre, built by the Greeks, modified by the Romans and still in use, was sited to take advantage of the view out to sea. A small museum houses finds from the site including a colossal head of Augustus. Nearby visit the sanctuary of the Black Madonna, a pilgrimage favourite. Map 2

A Morning Walk Around Cefalù

Start your walk at Piazza Garibaldi, beginning at Corso Ruggiero, where the church of Santa Maria della Catena is built on top of the 5th-century-BC town walls. Walking down the Corso, on the left at the corner of Via Amendola is one of the only extant parts of Norman Cefalù, besides the cathedral, the Palazzo Osterio Magno. Pass the flower-filled piazzetta in front of the Chiesa del Purgatorio on your way to Piazza Duomo, which opens up to the right. Inside the **cathedral** (see p44) admire the mosaics, but don't miss the exterior view of the apse around the back. Sit out in the piazza at Bar Duomo with a *cappuccino* and enjoy the cathedral façade and the church bells marking the hour.

Continue down the Corso to the end, take a left on Via Bordonaro and a right into Piazza Crispi with views of the Greek walls later absorbed by Spanish fortifications. Follow Via Bordonaro down to Piazza Marina with the small port below. Off to the left, down the Via Vittorio Emanuele, a staircase leads to *lavatoi* (washbasins), the sole remnant of Arab domination.

Before lunch, enjoy a wander around the "real" Cefalù, where fishermen repair boats and women pause from their laundry to chat.

Have lunch in the garden at Il Normanno (Via Vanni 9, close to Corso Ruggero • 0921 9259 03) or pick up picnic supplies from Alimentari e Salumeria Gatta Gaetano (Corso Ruggero 152).

Following pages: **Cefalù cathedral**

 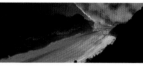

Left **Sulphur emissions** Right **Lava flow**

TOP 10 Mount Etna Eruptions

1 693 BC
A massive eruption destroyed the Greek settlement at Katane (ancient Catania).

2 396 BC
Lava flows from this eruption reached the Ionian Sea, preventing the Carthaginian Himilco from landing and thus stopping him from marching on Syracuse.

3 1169, 1329 and 1381
Eruptions in these three years sent lava all the way to the sea. The first arrived at Aci Castello; the last flowed all the way to Catania, pouring into the sea at Ognina and covering the Portus Ulixis, mentioned by Virgil in the epic poem *The Aeneid*.

4 1669
The worst eruption in modern times was preceded by three days of earthquakes. On the third day, a crevice 14 km (8.5 miles) long opened from the summit to Nicolosi and disgorged quantities of ash, rocks and lava. The eruption lasted four months, destroying several towns and leaving 27,000 people homeless.

5 1886
Lava flows from this eruption once again threatened the village of Nicolosi, but the veil of St Agatha was carried in a procession and the lava miraculously stopped. It was not the first time that St Agatha had purportedly halted a lava flow.

6 1911
Two major eruptions on the north side created a 5-km- (3-mile-) long crevice and 170 temporary craters. This crevice opened up again in 1923.

7 1928
A huge eruption destroyed the town of Mascali and a significant amount of cultivated land and buildings. It is the only time during the 20th century that a village was destroyed.

8 1979
An explosion killed nine tourists who were on the edge of the main crater, then poured lava into the Valle del Bove and almost reached Fornazzo.

9 1991–3
Lava flowed down the Valle del Bove towards Zafferana Etnea; authorities tried to divert the flow with explosives and by dropping concrete blocks from helicopters. The lava stopped just 1 km (half a mile) from the village.

10 2001–2
The most complex eruption in 300 years took place in 2001, when Etna disgorged ash and lava from six openings on the north and southeast sides, destroying the Etna Sud cablecar station. The 2002 eruption was no better, with visitors' centres and hotels destroyed. Some roads and Catania airport had to be closed both years.

For more details on Etna **See pp16–7**

Left **Boating** Right **Horse riding**

TOP 10 Outdoor Activities

1 Hiking, Madonie
The Madonie mountains are crisscrossed with marked trails graded for difficulty; several trails are suitable for the disabled. The trail map is available from the park service, tourist offices of larger towns within the park system, or from the tourist office in Palermo. The Italian Alpine Club organizes guided excursions. ◈ *Italian Alpine Club: 0921 641 028, www.cai.it*

2 Horse Riding, Madonie
The trails of the Madonie can be used by horse riders too. There are various riding stables, some annexed to good restaurants. ◈ *Ranch San Guglielmo: Castelbuono; 0921 671 150 • Rifugio Francesco Crispi: Castelbuono; 0921 672 279*

3 Hiking, Aeolian Islands
You can hike up the slopes to Vulcano's crater following the signs *"al cratere"*. Take a guide from the hydrofoil dock up the active volcano Stromboli.

4 Swimming, Aeolian Islands
Good swimming abounds in the Aeolians – the water is clear and rich in marine life.

5 Boating, Aeolian Islands
The best way to visit hidden coves and grottoes, and the only way to get from island to island, is by boat. Take your pick from a wide selection of organized tours from docks on any of the seven islands. Boat rentals are also available.

6 Walking, Tindari
Below the promontory, from Capo Tindari towards Oliveri and Falcone, the Tindari-Oliveri reserve is good for a quiet walk along the sand formations and lakes with blue-green water.

7 Hiking, Nebrodi
The Nebrodi Mountain Park encompasses protected yew and beech woods, pastureland, a wetlands habitat for migratory birds, birds of prey and wild horses. The park includes 21 villages where artisans produce goods and food. There are marked trails for hiking.

8 Alcantara Gorge
The Alcantara River runs at the bottom of a 20-m- (65-ft-) deep basalt gorge. From the car park, with waders for rent, walk down or take the lift to the bottom, where you can hike between the narrow walls and over waterfalls.

9 Hiking, Mount Etna
Ascend to the main crater or hike the slopes accompanied by a guide. ◈ *Gruppo Guide Alpine Etna Sud: 095 791 47 55; www.etnaguide.eu • Gruppo Guide Alpine Etna Nord: 095 777 45 02; www.guidetnanord.com*

10 Skiing, Mount Etna
There are about 10 ski runs on Etna. Lift tickets and equipment rentals are available.
◈ *Etna Sud Ski School: 349 178 71 38*
• Etna Nord Ski School: 347 655 17 93
• Etna Nord Snowboarding: 340 748 38 33
• www.scuolaitalianascietna.com

For more on active holidays **See p131**

Left **Mount Etna souvenirs** Right **Designer boutiques**

🔟 Specialist Shops and Markets

1 Mount Etna Souvenirs
The best in lava kitsch can be found at the base of Etna Sud or Etna Nord. Ashtrays, mini statues and animal figures – you name it, it has been moulded from molten lava and dipped in blue glitter. There are also more subdued trinkets, literature and videos of eruptions. ◈ *Map G3*

2 'A Putia, Giardini-Naxos
A vast array of delicious Sicilian products, including wine, cheese, honey, pistachios and preserves. There is also a restaurant. ◈ *Via Umberto 456 and Via IV Novembre 249 • Map H3*

3 Markets
Small street markets spring up in villages on Mount Etna's slopes. Local farmers offer their produce for sale from their cars and three-wheeled pick-up trucks, many near Fleri, between Viagrande and Santa Venerina.

4 Via Etnea, Catania
This district is famed for big-name Italian stores such as Max Mara, Benetton, Rinascente, Frette, as well as inviting pastry shops and cafés. Emporio Armani and other designer boutiques continue on the Corso Italia. ◈ *Map G4*

5 Le Colonne, Taormina
The proprietor of this jewellery store in Taormina creates pieces from old stones, inspired by historical motifs; she also works on commission if you create your own design. ◈ *Corso Umberto I, 164 • Map H3*

6 Apicoltura Privitera, Gravina di Catania
Located just above Catania, this shop sells honey, wine, mead, honey vinegar, propolis and soaps. They also sell online and can ship a bit of Sicily directly to your home. ◈ *Via Nino Martoglio 33 • Map G4*

7 Ceramiche dell'Artigianato Siciliano di Managò, Taormina
Signor Managò's Sicilian ceramics include designs from Caltagirone and Santo Stefano di Camastra. ◈ *Piazza San Domenico 1/2 • Map H3*

8 Fratelli Laise, Lipari
This store's booty of Aeolian goods includes capers, sundried tomatoes, honey, oregano and wine. ◈ *Via Vittorio Emanuele 188 • Map G1*

9 La Torinese, Taormina
Here since 1936, La Torinese sells top-quality wines and other tasty items such as liqueurs, tuna roe, salami, honey and olive oil. ◈ *Corso Umberto I, 59 • Map H3*

10 Ceramics, Santo Stefano di Camastra
Shops selling Santo Stefano's famous orange-and-yellow ceramics abound at this little town on the sea. ◈ *Map F2*

Price Categories

For a three-course
meal for one with half
a bottle of wine (or
equivalent meal), taxes
and extra charges.

€ under €25
€€ €25–€35
€€€ €35–€55
€€€€ €55–€70
€€€€€ over €70

Above **La Capinera**

🔟 Places to Eat

1 La Capinera, Taormina

Pietro d'Agostino's seaside restaurant is renowned for its amazingly creative fresh fish preparations, fair prices and beautiful atmosphere. ◈ *Via Nazionale 177, Spisone, Taormina Mare • Map H3 • 0942 626 247 • Closed Mon • €€€€€*

2 Osteria Nero d'Avola, Taormina

Chef Turi has been called an "ambassador for small artisan estates", and this shows on both his menu and his wine list. Great atmosphere and good prices *(see p77)*. ◈ *Piazza San Domenico 2b • Map H3 • 0942 628 874 • €€€*

3 Chalet Clan dei Ragazzi, Linguaglossa

This rustic wooden chalet, set at 1,500 m (4,900 ft) up Etna's northern slope, serves simple, authentic food. Book in advance for dinner. ◈ *Pineta Ragabo • Map G3 • 095 643 611 • No credit cards • €*

4 Ristorante Nenzyna, Lipari

This tiny *trattoria* near the port has a bright-blue façade. The owner is a grandmother who has been preparing the menu of fresh fish and other Aeolian Island favourites for more than 40 years. ◈ *Via Roma 2 • Map G1 • 090 981 1660 • Closed Nov–Easter • €€*

5 Trattoria da Pina, Vulcano

Good Aeolian cuisine is served on a dockside terrace at Gelso, with views all the way to Mount Etna. ◈ *Gelso • Map G1*

• 368 668 555 • No credit cards • Closed mid-Oct–Easter • €€

6 La Grotta, Acireale

An actual grotto, this six-table restaurant is a local favourite thanks to the excellence of the fish. Booking is a must. ◈ *Via Scalo Grande 46, Santa Maria La Scala • Map G3 • 095 764 81 53 • Closed Tue • €€€*

7 Osteria Antica Marina, Catania

This *osteria* in the middle of the fish market sells a selection of each day's catch. Try the marinated anchovies. ◈ *Via Pardo 29 • Map G4 • 095 348 197 • Closed Wed • €€*

8 Pepe Rosa, Bronte

Bronte is renowned for its pistachios, and they are featured in every course at this charming little family-run restaurant. Be sure not to miss the *bruschetta* with pistachio pesto. ◈ *Corso Umberto 226 • Map G3 • 095 772 44 76 • Closed Mon • €€*

9 Ristorante Pizzeria Granduca, Taormina

This terraced pizzeria has a garden and wonderful views. ◈ *Corso Umberto 172 • Map H3 • 094 224 983 • Closed Tue (Nov–Apr) • €€€*

10 Nangalarruni, Castelbuono

Great mountain food cooked with quality ingredients, such as pork from the Nebrodi heritage breed. ◈ *Via delle Confraternite 7 • Map E3 • 092 167 14 28 • Closed Wed (except Jul–mid-Sep) • €€€*

> **Note:** Unless otherwise stated, all restaurants accept credit cards and serve vegetarian meals.

Left **Prizzi, Il Corleonese** Right **Palazzo Adriano, Il Corleonese**

Southwest Sicily

THE BEAUTY OF SOUTHWEST SICILY *lies even beyond the splendid mosaics of the Villa Romana and the temples at Agrigento. Sandy beaches, lovely fishing villages, ruined Greek cities and silvery olive and dark green citrus groves feature all along the little-developed coastline. Enna dominates the wide, wheat-filled valleys, while small farming villages of the unspoiled interior remain isolated on their hilltops, with vast expanses of rocky mountains or rolling fields between them. Because of the lack of infrastructure, the area remained remote until well into the 19th century, then mass emigration slowed modern development in the 20th century. As a result, these little villages have remained almost as they were centuries ago, a testimony to Sicily's agrarian past.*

🔟 Sights

1. Villa Romana del Casale
2. Agrigento and the Valle dei Templi
3. Il Corleonese
4. Sciacca
5. Enna
6. Caltabellotta
7. Morgantina
8. Eraclea Minoa
9. Badia di Santo Spirito, Caltanissetta
10. Pelagie Islands

Morgantina

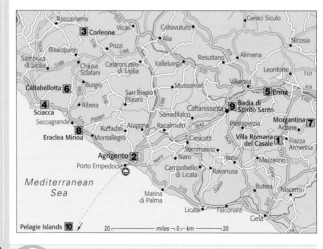

1 Villa Romana del Casale

The finest surviving Roman mosaics in the world cover the floors of this official's luxurious hunting villa *(see pp24–5)*.

2 Agrigento and the Valle dei Templi

The Valley of the Temples was the heart of one of the most important cities in the ancient world and is a prime example of the magnificence of Magna Graecia *(see pp26–9)*.

3 Il Corleonese

The central zone around the village of Corleone *(see p49)* is referred to as *il Corleonese* and has long been known for its generous water supplies and fertile soil – driving through the countryside, the richness of the land is evident. Small, remote villages are sprinkled throughout, all worth a quick visit to witness a way of life that is slow to change. Among them, visit Prizzi, Bisacquino, Palazzo Adriano, Cammarata, Mussomeli and Corleone itself, a successful modern town with a lovely historic centre. ◈ *Map C3*

4 Sciacca

Dominated by Monte San Calogero and built on a terrace over the sea, this was the thermal spa town for Selinunte and still has a spa offering restorative sulphur and mud baths. The small port town has an interesting harbour choked with little blue-and-white boats, a thriving ceramics tradition and a good mix of old and new. See the Porta San Salvatore (1581), carved by local artisans with carpet-like decorative reliefs, and the Catalan-Gothic Palazzo Steripinto, with its diamond-shaped rustication. Then walk the

Palazzo Steripinto, Sciacca

Corso Vittorio Emanuele to the Piazza A Scandaliato for views down to the port, then on to the Duomo for its Baroque façade with Gagini sculptures. ◈ *Map C4*

5 Enna

Due to its easily defendable position on the top of a tall hill, Enna was almost the only town in the interior for centuries. The Greeks called it the "umbilicus of Sicily", and it was a key position for any group that wanted to take the island. Enna was so well defended that the Arabs, having tried to capture it for 20 years, resorted to crawling in through the sewer system. In the historic centre, see the Gothic Duomo with Baroque renovations and the church of San Giovanni with an Arab dome. Also visit the Museo Musical Art 3M. It's hard to miss Frederick's Tower, once considered Sicily's geographical centre. Built in the mid-13th century, it is 24 m (79 ft) tall and octagonal in shape, with fine views from the top. Castello di Lombardia is one of the largest and most important of Sicily's medieval castles. It is a mixture of Byzantine, Arab, Norman and Swabian architecture.

Don't miss the lively afternoon fish market in Sciacca – it starts around 2pm.

6 Caltabellotta

This tiny village, 950 m (3,100 ft) above sea level, has a lovely medieval centre. In 1090, the already fortified village was taken from the Arabs by the Norman king Count Roger, who built the Chiesa Madre and fortified the now ruined castle. It was in this castle in 1194 that William III, heir to the Norman throne, and his mother were imprisoned and probably murdered by Emperor Henry VI; it was also the site of the signing of the 1302 peace treaty between Frederick II of Aragón and Charles of Valois, putting an end to the Sicilian Vespers *(see pp36–7)*. ◈ *Map C4*

7 Morgantina

Morgantina was settled first by the Italic Morganti people, then by the Greeks in the 6th century BC, then the Romans, but it was only excavated in 1955. The extensive, well-preserved site comprises a split-level *agora* (forum) connected by a 14-step staircase that served as the site of town meetings, the *macellum* (covered market), a gymnasium, a public fountain with a double basin, large black

Cliff, Eraclea Minoa

lava millstones, residences with mosaic flooring, a 1,000-seat theatre, an enormous public granary and kilns for firing terracotta. The larger of the two kilns was also used for firing construction materials. ◈ *Map F4* • *Open 9am–1 hour before sunset daily* • *Adm*

8 Eraclea Minoa

Above vineyards and olive groves thriving in the rocky soil and on the white sandstone cliffs, the ruins of this ancient Greek city lie on a headland above a wide sandy beach. Midway between Selinunte and Agrigento and on the border between Carthaginian- and Greek-held territory, Eraclea Minoa saw its fair share of border disputes. The site is quiet now, and well kept. A small museum and groomed paths lead to an intimate theatre carved into the sandstone, remains of defensive walls with towers and the residential section where a few houses made of local stone preserve their floor and wall decorations. Since it's not on the standard tour bus route, the added pleasure of a visit is that you may have this gorgeous place all to yourself. ◈ *Map C4* • *Open summer: 9am–7pm daily* • *Adm*

Oranges and Other Citrus Fruits

Citrus fruits were introduced to Sicily by the Arabs and have been an important cash crop for centuries. There are lemons, both sharp and sweet, tangerines, mandarins and endless varieties of oranges, from sweet to sour, from pale gold to dark purple. The plantations, plentiful particularly in the zone around Ribera, are characteristic for their low-growing trees with dark-green leaves, bright fruits and heady fragrance *(la zagara)*.

9 Badia di Santo Spirito, Caltanissetta

The Abbey of the Holy Spirit was founded around 1090 by Count Roger and his wife, Adelasia, and consecrated in 1153. It is one of the few Romanesque Norman buildings to remain intact. The exterior is unadorned except for the portals and the small, triple apse articulated with tall, narrow arcading. The interior contains 14th- and 15th-century frescoes and a dedicatory inscription dating from 1153 in the apse.
Ⓢ Map E4 • Open 9am–noon, 4–7pm daily • Free

10 Pelagie Islands

The three flat islands that form this group are romantically isolated in the middle of the Mediterranean. Lampione is uninhabited, while Linosa is known for its fertile, volcanic soil and crystal-clear waters. Lampedusa, the largest of the three, responded to a tourism boom with modern buildings, but is still good for swimming, diving and watching sea turtles, dolphins and whales (they migrate in March). The coast of Lampedusa was the object of the 1987 Libyan missile strike that fell short, dumping missiles into the sea. Ⓢ Map B6

Lampedusa, Pelagie Islands

An Afternoon in Caltabellotta

🕐 Take a late afternoon drive from Sciacca up to **Caltabellotta**. Skip the modern outskirts of town to wander around the narrow streets and *piazzettas* of Terravecchia, the old medieval centre. Terravecchia lies on a flat plain under the Chiesa Madre founded by Count Roger one year before he took Palermo *(see pp8–9)*. It has been restored, so admire the entry portal with pointed arch and the bell tower which was originally an old Arabic fortification; inside see the *Madonna of the Chain*, *St Benedict* and *Madonna and Child* – all works by the artist Gagini.

To the north of the church, take the little path up the rock to the ruins of the Castelvecchio, the old castle, from which you can look down on Caltabellotta and out over the valley.

On the other side of the plain, opposite the Chiesa Madre, find the tiny church of San Salvatore with its zigzag decoration around the door. Use the steps carved out of the rock to climb up to the highest point of Monte Castello. Walk around the ruins of Count Roger's castle, with its single Gothic doorway, and take in one of the most stunning views in Sicily. To the southwest see the coastline from **Agrigento** *(see pp26–9)* to **Marsala** *(see p92)*.

Back in town, stroll from Piazza Umberto I to Via Roma in the newer part of the village, where you can have an excellent dinner of mountain fare at **La Ferla** trattoria *(see p115)*.

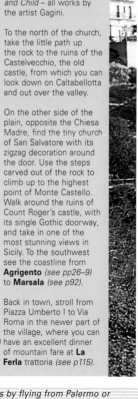

➲ You can get to the Pelagie Islands by flying from Palermo or Catania, or taking a ferry from Porto Empedocle.

Left **Sicilian citrus fruits** Right **Ceramics**

TOP 10 Local Produce

1 Wine
During the 20th century large estates planted with wheat and other crops started planting vines to produce high-quality wine. Two examples are Regaleali near Vallelunga and Planeta near Sambuca di Sicilia.

2 Co-operative Produce
In and around Corleone *(see p49)*, several co-operatives under the umbrella *Libera Terra* cultivate land confiscated from Mafia bosses to create jobs and strengthen the economy of the area. Wheat is grown for pasta, grapes for wine, as well as fruits, cheeses and honey.

3 Oranges
Ribera is known for its production of the prized Washington variety of navel orange, introduced to the area by emigrants returning from North America.

4 Artichokes
A staple of Sicilian cuisine, they are at their best in spring. The town of Cerda celebrates the artichoke each April, with a three-day festival at which they are cooked and served in every possible way.

5 Olive Oil
One of Sicily's biggest and most popular exports. Cities such as Castelvetrano and Trapani are famous for their olives. The harvest begins in October, and the first pressings of the new extra virgin olive oil are bottled and available from the end of November onwards. Many towns celebrate the arrival of the new season's oil with tastings.

6 Fresh Fish
Fishing villages line the southern coast of Sicily, with important centres at Licata, Porto Empedocle and Sciacca.

7 Preserved Fish
Preserved tuna was a staple food for centuries on ships sailing the Mediterranean, and tuna as well as anchovies and sardines are still big business. At Sciacca, anchovies and sardines are processed by hand and packed under salt or olive oil for export all over the world.

8 Wheat
The interior of the island was taken up with *latifondi* until well into the 20th century, and it's still an important source of income. Vast valleys and hills are devoted to cultivating Sicily's special *grano duro (see p70)*.

9 Ceramics
Traditional ceramics are still made in various centres, notably Sciacca, where the designs are in green, yellow and blue.

10 Broad Beans
Large broad beans, or *fave*, are cultivated in the countryside near Enna. They are eaten dressed with olive oil or used in soups.

Left **Prizzi** Right **Enna valley**

TOP 10 Scenic Views

1 From Caltabellota
From the ruins of the Norman castle above Caltabellotta *(see p110)* you can see all the way to the flat coast stretching toward Marsala and the hilly interior dotted with villages and farms. ◎ *Map C4*

2 The Valle dei Templi by Night
Agrigento's temples are even more romantic at night. You can see them from any vantage point, but perhaps the finest view is from the terrace at Il Dehors, enjoying an excellent meal with the Temple of Concord as backdrop *(see pp26–9)*.

3 Prizzi
Driving through the Corleonese zone *(see p109)*, Prizzi is one of the highest towns, covering the top of its hill like a *cobbola* (peasant farmer's cap). ◎ *Map D3*

4 Views from Enna
From the Piazza Cripsi, see across the deep valley to Calascibetta on the flat top of its own terraced hill, and across the interior all the way to Mount Etna. ◎ *Map E4*

5 Enna
From the valley floor to the east, Enna presents an impressive sight, the Rock of Demeter dominating the cliff above the site where Persephone was abducted by Hades *(see p109)*.

6 Countryside around Corleone and Prizzi
Vast expanses of rolling terrain are planted with wheat, vines, olives and silvery blue artichokes. Colours pop up here and there amid the green, such as a large swathe of crimson sulla, bright-red poppies and hearty yellow fennel growing impossibly tall *(see p109)*.

7 Vallate near Enna
The enormous *vallate* (valleys) around Enna are planted with wheat, and the spectacular stretches of soft fields change colour with the seasons, from lush green, to golden yellow, to black. ◎ *Map E4*

8 The Rocca di Nadore
The round-topped Rocca di Nadore above Sciacca turns its flat, white face towards the sea and dominates the coast for miles. See it looming on the horizon as far away as Selinunte. ◎ *Map C4*

9 From Morgantina
From the residential sector on the east hill, look down on the *agora* (forum) and out towards the east coast and the outline of Mount Etna *(see p110)*.

10 From Eraclea Minoa
From the ruins of Eraclea Minoa on top of a white sandstone cliff, look down to the wide stretch of sandy beach and the dark sea *(see p110)*.

Left **Lago di Pergusa** Right **Enna**

Chthonic Deities and their Sites

Demeter
The cult of the Mother Goddess, protector of agriculture and fertility, is one of the most ancient in Sicily. When her daughter Persephone disappeared, Demeter roamed the earth searching for her, ignoring crops, and thus allowing the earth to become wrought with famine.

Persephone
The daughter of Demeter and Zeus (also known as Kore or, to the Romans, Proserpine) rules as both Queen of the Underworld and Goddess of Fertility.

Persephone's Abduction
While gathering lilies, violets and hyacinths with her girlfriends in fields below Enna, Persephone was abducted by Hades and taken to reign as Queen of the Underworld.

Persephone's Return to Earth
Hades agreed to release Persephone on condition that she ate a pomegranate seed (food of the dead), so ensuring her return to the Underworld for four months each year. When she reigns in the Underworld, it is winter on Earth; when she returns, she brings spring and renewal.

Lago di Pergusa
A deep natural lake south of Enna is the supposed site of the passage from Earth to the Underworld.

Sanctuary at Enna
The seat of the cult of Demeter and Persephone was at Enna on the boulder behind the castle. Their temple contained a statue of the Mother Goddess.

Votive Offerings from the Sanctuary at Enna
Items recovered from the sanctuary and from sites near Lake Pergusa are preserved in Enna's Museo Archeologico, including votive statuettes of Demeter. ◎ *Museo Archeologico, Palazzo Varisano, Piazza Mazzini • Map E4 • Open 9am– 6:30pm daily • Adm*

Rock Sanctuary of Demeter, Agrigento
The earth goddesses were venerated at a sanctuary now marked by the church of San Biagio. The church was built on top of a 5th-century BC temple; two round altars are extant *(see p27)*.

Sanctuary at Morgantina
Demeter and Persephone were worshipped as the protectors of Morgantina. In the sanctuary see purification baths, altars for performing rituals and a well for sacred offerings.

Sanctuary at Palma di Montechiaro
Three 7th-century-BC votive statuettes of Demeter or Persephone, now in Syracuse's archaeological museum, were recovered from this sanctuary between Agrigento and Gela.

Above **Trattoria dei Templi**

Price Categories

For a three-course meal for one with half a bottle of wine (or equivalent meal), taxes and extra charges.

€	under €25
€€	€25–€35
€€€	€35–€55
€€€€	€55–€70
€€€€€	over €70

🔟 Places to Eat

1 La Madia, Licata
Chef Pino Cuttaia's creativity and dedication to seasonality make this small restaurant worth a trip to Licata *(see p76).*
🔷 *Corso Re F Capriata 22 • Map E5 • 0922 771 443 • Closed Tue, Sun dinner; Sun lunch (Jul & Aug) • €€€€€*

2 Ristorante Pomara, San Michele di Ganzaria
The restaurant centres around the stone fireplace where local cheeses, vegetables and meats are grilled to accompany hearty dishes such as pasta with pistachios. 🔷 *Via Vittorio Veneto 84 • Map F4 • 0933 978 032 • €€*

3 La Ferla, Caltabellota
A local favourite with a terrace and sea views. Try the roasted artichokes and local cheeses. 🔷 *Via Roma 29 • Map C4 • 0925 951 444 • Closed Mon, Oct • €€*

4 Ruga Reali, Agrigento
An informal *osteria* popular with locals and specializing in fish dishes. The 15th-century building has wooden beams and a courtyard for alfresco dining.
🔷 *Piazza Pirandello 9 (Cortile Scribani 8) • Map D4 • 0922 20 370 • Closed Sun • €€*

5 Trattoria La Vecchia Conza, Sciacca Terme
In a charming interior with rustic decor, traditional local dishes are served on elaborately decorated, locally crafted ceramic plates.
🔷 *Via P Gerardi 37/39 • Map C4 • 0925 25 385 • Closed Mon, Nov • €€*

6 Porto San Paolo, Sciacca
Come here for a menu prepared with the daily catch, either cooked or sushi-style. Terrace tables look over Sciacca's small port and out to sea. 🔷 *Largo San Paolo 1 • Map C4 • 0925 27 982 • Closed Wed, mid-Oct–mid-Nov • €€€*

7 La Lanterna, Milena
An informal *trattoria* serving authentic, traditional Sicilian food using fresh, local produce, and offering a good-value set menu.
🔷 *Via Pietro Nenni 8 • Map D4 • 0934 933 478 • Closed Mon • €€*

8 Antica Stazione Ferroviaria di Ficuzza, near Corleone
Enjoy traditional fare of inland Sicily, prepared with quality ingredients, many supplied by local organic producers. 🔷 *Via Stazione, Ficuzza • Map C3 • 091 846 0000 • €€*

9 Trattoria dei Templi, Agrigento
This family-run *trattoria* has a reputation for its Sicilian menu: try the pasta with swordfish and mint. 🔷 *Via Panoramica dei Templi 15 • Map D4 • 0922 403 110 • Closed Sun (Jun–Sep), Fri (winter) • €€€*

10 Capitolo Primo del Relais Briuccia, Montallegro, near Agrigento
Creative versions of Sicilian dishes that make use of the island's varied aromas, ranging from wild fennel to saffron, are served here.
🔷 *Via Trieste 1 • Map D4 • 339 759 2176 • Closed Mon • €€€*

Note: *Unless otherwise stated, all restaurants accept credit cards and serve vegetarian meals.*

Left **Palazzolo Acreide** Right **Noto beach**

Southeast Sicily

THE LANDSCAPE OF THE SOUTHEAST IS MARKEDLY DIFFERENT *from the rest of the island*, with its strata of white limestone supporting scrubland vegetation, steep gorges formed by ancient river courses, and characteristic low, dry-stone walls marking the boundaries of fertile fields. Yet this small corner of Sicily is rich in sights. Unmissable are the Greek and Roman remains at Syracuse, the most important city of Magna Graecia, while Caltagirone, Modica, Noto, Palazzolo Acreide, Ragusa and Scicli have all recently been declared World Heritage Sites on the merits of their Baroque architecture and innovative urban planning, the result of the rebuilding effort after the destruction of the 1693 earthquake. Of equal enjoyment is the current gastronomic renaissance taking place in the area, rediscovering both the seafood from the coastal zones and the meats, cheeses and wild greens of the interior. Young chefs, aware that old traditions, methods and even ingredients are on the brink of extinction, are returning to their roots and working hard to revitalize and preserve the authentic cuisine of the region.

San Domenico, Noto

Sights

1. Syracuse
2. Noto
3. Ragusa Ibla
4. Modica
5. Scicli
6. Palazzolo Acreide
7. Southeast Plains
8. Caltagirone
9. Grammichele
10. Pantalica Necropolis

Syracuse

Remains of the mighty powerhouse of Magna Graecia make up some of the most important sites in Sicily, while the small historic centre of Ortygia *(see p124)* is one of the most pleasant town centres on the island *(see pp18–21)*.

Noto

Noto is the chief proponent of the new cities built entirely in Baroque style after the 1693 earthquake destroyed most of eastern Sicily. Noto was rebuilt using a tufa stone that has turned a golden shade after years of sun, while the architecture is ebullient and dramatic. The town plan involves open, wide streets with plenty of piazzas and *piazzettas* for gathering and making the *passeggiata (see pp22–3)*.

Ragusa Ibla

Ragusa was founded as Hybla Heraia by Siculi peoples fleeing inland to escape the Greeks. After the earthquake of 1693, half the population chose to rebuild on the ridge above (Ragusa), while the other half chose to renovate the old village (Ragusa Ibla). Ibla makes an immediate impression with its little terracotta roof-tiled buildings clinging dramatically to the side of a cliff. The Duomo is at the heart of town, sited on a rise to emphasize its great height. A Gagliardi masterpiece of 1744, the façade is articulated with a pulsating entablature, bulging columns and swirling volutes pushing upwards toward the tall central bell tower. The oval-shaped cathedral of San Giuseppe presents another projecting Baroque façade. Also not to be missed is the surviving portal of the pre-quake cathedral, Catalan-Gothic in style and with a delicately carved St George slaying the dragon. ◈ *Map F5*

Modica

Rebuilt after 1693, on and between two deep gorges, the city is dramatically divided in two parts – Modica Alta, the upper town, and Modica Bassa, the lower town. Founded by the Siculi, the city attained great importance under Spanish rule, when it was the capital of a quasi-autonomous state ruled by Spanish barons. The lively Corso Umberto I, with boutiques, cafés, pastry shops, numerous palaces and a theatre, crosses Modica Bassa. Also on this street is a monumental flight of steps with excellent Baroque statues of the Apostles that leads up to the post-1693 Duomo dedicated to San Pietro. Up the hill, Modica Alta's Baroque church of San Giorgio is attributed to Gagliardi. Inside, there is characteristic stucco work and 10 beautiful 16th-century wooden panels depicting scenes from the New Testament. ◈ *Map G6*

Ragusa Ibla

Scicli

5 Dominated by a high, rocky cliff, Scicli was an outpost of the Spanish barons during their long reign over the County of Modica. From the wide Piazza Italia, the via Nazionale leads up to the west, passing the side street where the Palazzo Beneventano sits on a corner, its sculptural decoration now weathered by the elements. Via Nazionale continues to the pleasant Piazza Busacca, with views down into the older, residential section of town with its narrow lanes and crumbling terracotta roofs. ◉ *Map F6*

Palazzolo Acreide

6 The "modern" Baroque town was originally a Greek colony of Syracuse, founded in 664 BC. At the archaeological site just next to the village, the small, 600-seat Greek theatre remains in good condition, although temples to Persephone and Aphrodite are in ruins. Old quarries bear a Greek banqueting scene and a Roman sacrifice carved in relief. A short walk outside the old city are the *Santoni* (Big Saints), enormous statues of fertility goddess Cybele and her entourage carved out of the rock (*see p49*). ◉ *Map G5*

Carob Trees

Enormous *carrubi* (carob trees) are a characteristic feature of southeast Sicily. The trees produce a fruit shaped like a brown pea pod, with sweet flesh and hard seeds. The seeds are amazingly uniform and were the original karat used to weigh precious stones. Carob's sweet flesh can be used in pasta and sweets. Once called "poor man's chocolate", the deep, rich flavour is now prized by the best chefs of the region.

Caltagirone

Southeast Plains

7 On the upland plain around Ragusa and Modica the soil is marked with white stone outcroppings and gorges, while, on the lowland plain around Vittoria, the tufa lies almost 1 m (3 ft) below the surface and is topped with a layer of red soil that supports bright-green grapevines. Pastures crisscrossed with walls are marked by stone *masserie* (farmer's homes). The farmer (*massaro*) works the fields, raises livestock and produces grain, olive oil and milk for the local *caciocavallo Ragusano* cheese.

Caltagirone

8 Named after the Arabic *Cal'at Ghiran* (Castle of Vases), ceramic production has been the main industry in this town since prehistoric times, a tradition documented at the local Museo della Ceramica. The Baroque town built onto a steep hillside is a pleasure to wander through, with characteristic alleyways, cafés and ceramics shops. A stairway leads from the lower town up to the church of Santa Maria del Monte, and each of the 142 steps is decorated with majolica tiles. ◉ *Map F4*

Grammichele

9 Built by the Principe di Butera after the 1693 earthquake to house the farmers of the destroyed village of Occhiolà, this lovely place preserves an authentic peasant-farmer feel, even though it was built on a grand plan inspired by Renaissance mathematical ideals. The concentric hexagonal plan radiates from around the central Piazza Umberto I, home to private residences, *palazzi*, the Chiesa Madre and the town hall. ◈ *Map F5*

Pantalica Necropolis

10 Pantalica was at the heart of ancient Hybla, the culture known now only through its striking red glazed pottery, examples of which are on view in Syracuse. The Anapo River carved a steep gorge through the limestone creating what became Sicily's largest necropolis; there are more than 8,000 tombs here. A hike through the gorge takes you past thousands of burial sites, carved into the cliff sides, as well as remains of a medieval settlement, wild orchids, irises, rabbits, porcupines, falcons, trout and crabs. ◈ *Map G5*

Pantalica Necropolis

A Day in Modica and Ragusa Ibla

Morning

🕑 Spend a morning in **Modica** *(see p117)*, stopping by the church of San Giorgio of Modica Alta on your way into town. In Modica Bassa, visit the equally splendid Sicilian Baroque church of San Pietro. Walk down the Corso Umberto I towards the Duomo, passing cafés, shops and buildings that incorporate parts of pre-earthquake structures. At Corso Umberto I, 156, visit the *biscottificio* of Donna Elvira Roccasalva *(see p74)* and, at 159, Dolceria Bonajuto, the oldest chocolate factory in Sicily, to taste and buy a wide range of Modica's traditional sweets.

Drive along the SS 115 to **Ragusa Ibla** *(see p117)* crossing one of the tallest viaducts in Europe into a fertile land of citrus groves and carob trees. In Giardini Iblei, pick up a map of the maze-like streets from the information office. Next door, have lunch at **Ristorante Duomo** *(see p125)*.

Afternoon

Spend the afternoon wandering through Ragusa Ibla to see the Duomo di San Giorgio and San Giuseppe. You can study the Baroque façade of the Duomo from under the trees in the lively piazza with a treat from Gelati DiVini (Piazza Duomo 20) – their ice cream is made from Sicilian wines. But don't fail to walk through the narrow side streets, where tiny alleys are connected with staircases and tunnels, for a taste of authentic Ibla.

Following pages: **Greek theatre, Syracuse**

Left **Castello Eurialo** Right **Villa Natalina, Modica**

🔟 Best of the Rest

1 Noto Antica
To the northwest of Noto lie the evocative ruins of the pre-earthquake town. Built on an arid, limestone ridge, the site commands views of the Ragusan plain and Mount Etna. Under the hot Sicilian sun, purple thistle and sun dried herbs perfume the air. 🚫 *Map G5*

2 Castello Eurialo
This Greek military castle was built in 402 BC and is notable for its 15-m (50-ft) keep. Spectacular views of the coastline can be had from its fortifications *(see p46).* 🚫 *Map G5 • Open 9am–5:30pm daily • Adm*

3 Giarratana
This tiny town in the middle of the Monte Iblei has narrow streets lined with palaces, churches and residences. Note the typical homes, with low doors, to protect against cold winter winds. 🚫 *Map G5*

4 Megara Iblea
Lovely and extensive coastal remains of a town founded in 728 BC by Greek colonists from Megara, near Athens. 🚫 *Map G5*

5 Ciane River
The river's source is a pool formed by the tears of Cyane, who tried to prevent Persephone's abduction into the Underworld. The river banks are thick with papyrus. Take a boat tour past the Olympieion. 🚫 *Map G5*

6 Vendicari
The reserve's maquis supports thyme, rosemary and juniper; the wetlands host migratory birds. Depending on the season, watch for herons, egrets and flamingoes. 🚫 *Map G6*

7 Cave d'Ispica
An ancient river carved out this gorge, which is now an open-air park with good walks and climbs. The cliff sides are hollowed out to form ancient tombs of religious hermits; in one cave is a Byzantine fresco of the Madonna. 🚫 *Map G6*

8 Marzamemi
This little fishing village grew up around the *tonnara* (tuna fishery) and villa of the noble Villadorata family. The old village remains, but with the addition of modern resort features, including popular nightclubs. 🚫 *Map G6*

9 Lentini
The excavations of this small former Greek colony, home to the philosopher Gorgias, are well worth exploring to get a sense of the power and importance that it once had. 🚫 *Map G4*

10 Sampieri
Clear waters and sandy beaches surround what was once a small fishing village. The beaches at Punta Pisciotto are accessed from a turn-off at the abandoned, temple-like brick kilns called Fornace Penna. 🚫 *Map F6*

Left **Casa-Museo di Antonino Uccello** Right **Museo del Tempo Contadino**

🔟 Ethnographic Museums

1 Museo del Tempo Contadino, Ragusa
The beautiful Palazzo Zacco houses a collection of historic farming and farmhouse kitchen tools, along with lovely lace and embroidery work. ◈ *Palazzo Zacco, Via San Vito 158 • Map F5 • Open 9am–1pm, 3:30–5:30pm Mon–Fri • Adm*

2 Museo della Civiltà Contadina Iblea, Floridia
Mills for wheat and olives, looms and a range of tools have been collected from farmers' homes throughout the Iblean countryside. ◈ *Piazza Umberto I, 27 • Map G5 • Open 5:30pm–8:30pm Mon–Fri • Adm*

3 Casa-Museo di Antonino Uccello, Palazzolo Acreide
Exhibits of Sicilian peasant farmers' hand-made objects *(see p39).* ◈ *Via Machiavelli 19, Palazzolo Acreide • Map G5 • Open 9am–7pm Mon–Sat, 2:30–7:30pm Sun • Adm*

4 Mulino ad Acqua Santa Lucia, Palazzolo Acreide
An antique water-powered grain mill has been put back into action, complete with working millstones. ◈ *Via Machiavelli 19 • Map G5 • Open 9am–1pm Mon–Sat • Adm*

5 Centro di Documentazione della Vita Popolare Iblea, Buscemi
The centre preserves 180 hours of film and 12,000 prints documenting agricultural life. ◈ *Via Vittorio Emanuele • Map G5 • Open 9am–1pm Mon–Sat • Adm*

6 I Luoghi del Lavoro Contadino, Buscemi
Buscemi is a living museum. Eight workrooms and living spaces, including the home of a peasant farmer, a smithy and a mill, have been faithfully preserved. ◈ *Via Libertà 10 • Map G5 • Open 9am–1pm daily • Adm*

7 Museo del Costume, Scicli
The museum is dedicated to keeping alive the history and culture of the Iblean mountain communities. ◈ *Cortile Opera Pia Carpintiera, Via Francesco Mormina Penna 65 • Map F6 • Open 6:30–11pm daily (also 10:30am–12:30pm Fri–Sun) • Free*

8 Museo del Ricamo e dello Sfilato, Chiaramonte Gulfi
Antique looms and instruments for the production of thread and cloth are on display here. ◈ *Via Laurea 4 • Map F5 • Open 8:30am–1pm Tue–Fri, 10am–1pm Sat & Sun • Adm*

9 A Casa do Fascitraru, Sortino
Sortino is renowned for its beekeeping tradition. This museum displays beekeeping and honey-making implements. ◈ *Via Gioberti 5 • Map G5 • Open by appt (tel: 0931 952 992) • Adm*

10 Museo di Civiltà Contadina Angelo Marsiano, Niscemi
Displays on life in the Sicilian countryside and traditional crafts. ◈ *Via Mazzini 78 • Map F5 • Open 10am–noon, 4–6pm in summer, or on request (tel: 0933 951 722) • Free*

Full-day tours of Buscemi include lunch and a visit to the Mulino ad Acqua Santa Lucia, in Palazzolo Acreide.

Left **Ortygia market** Right **Temple of Apollo**

10 Ortygia Sights

Ortygia
The tiny island is a bustling mix of temples, churches, museums, open piazzas, seaside bars, markets and shops. It also has a lively after-hours scene.

Temple of Apollo
On Largo XXV Luglio are the remains of the Doric Temple of Apollo. Built in 575 BC, this was the first temple in Sicily with an exterior colonnade of stone columns. Two monolithic sandstone columns remain.

Piazza del Duomo
Excavations in this square have unearthed the remains of 8th-century-BC houses belonging to the original Sicel culture. Around the oblong piazza are the Duomo, the town hall (located atop an Ionic Temple to Artemis) and outdoor cafés.

Duomo
One of the most spectacular buildings in Sicily, the dramatic Baroque façade fronts a 5th-century-BC Doric Temple to Athena. It was transformed into a church in the 7th century AD. Clearly visible inside and out are monolithic Doric columns.

Piazzetta San Rocco
This little piazza and the network of streets around it are the hub of Ortygia's night scene. It is definitely the place to come to kick-start a lively night.

Fonte Aretusa
The mythical Arethusa *(see p37)* was turned into a spring and bubbles up on the shores of lower Ortygia. Along the Lungomare Alfeo, a little terrace looks down on the spring that now feeds into a pond, with ducks and tall papyrus.

The Greek Ghetto
The six parallel streets between Via della Giudecca and Via GB Alagona follow the Greek urban plan. It is still crowded with medieval houses and laundry flapping in the breeze.

Castello Maniace
Frederick II built this castle around 1239. It takes its name from the Byzantine George Maniakes who "liberated" Syracuse in the 11th century.
Open 9am–1pm Tue–Sun • Adm

Market
The market typically bustles with local housewives and vendors yelling out the merits of their wares. Farmers and fishermen heap mussels, tomatoes, cherries or whatever is plentiful into colourful mounds to entice customers. Via Giaraca & Via Trento • Mon–Sat am

Via Maestranza
Now lined with boutiques and restaurants, this street was where noble families built their Baroque palaces, often incorporating older structures.

Enjoy the sunset on the Lungomare at the Fonte Aretusa.

Above **La Gazza Ladra**

Price Categories

For a three-course meal for one with half a bottle of wine (or equivalent meal), taxes and extra charges.	**€** under €25
	€€ €25–€35
	€€€ €35–€55
	€€€€ €55–€70
	€€€€€ over €70

🔟 Places to Eat

1 Ristorante Duomo, Ragusa Ibla

Ciccio Sultano expertly chooses local ingredients. The food is outstanding, served in an elegant dining room (see p76). ⊗ Via Capitano Bocchieri 31 • Map F5 • 0932 651 265 • Closed Sun, Lunch in Jan • €€€€€

2 Singola, Modica

Singola uses fresh seasonal ingredients from local farms, organic where possible, in its creative vegan dishes. There's a great atmosphere, as well. ⊗ Via Risorgimento 88 • Map G6 • 0932 904 807 • Closed Tue, Wed–Fri & Mon lunch • €€

3 Ristorante Fidone Maria, Frigintini

This family-run trattoria near Ragusa prepares everything in house, and it's all excellent (see p76). ⊗ Via Gianforma Margione 6 • Map F5 • 0932 901 135 • No credit cards • Dinner only; closed Mon (except Aug) • €€

4 La Gazza Ladra, Modica

Experience romantically named culinary creations in the historic setting of Palazzo Failla (see pp76–7). ⊗ Hotel Palazzo Failla, Via Blandini 11 • Map G6 • 0932 755 655 • Closed Sun dinner, Mon, Nov • €€€€€

5 Ristorante Crocifisso, Noto

This family-run restaurant offers recipes like coniglio stimperata (sweet and sour rabbit), fried ricotta, and ravioli in pork ragù. ⊗ Via Principe Umberto 48 • Map G5 • 0931 571 151 • Closed Wed • €€€

6 Sakalleo, Scoglitti

The menu depends upon what the owner's fishing boats bring in. The animated owner may also have a glass of wine with you. ⊗ Piazza Cavour 12 • Map F5 • 0932 871 688 • €€€

7 Majore, Chiaramonte Gulfi

"Quì si magnifica il porco" (Here the pig is glorified) is the motto of this restaurant, which is also a butcher's. ⊗ Via Martiri Ungheresi 12 • Map F5 • 0932 928 019 • Closed Mon • €€

8 Al Molo, Donnalucata

Sit on a veranda facing the wharf where fishermen sell their catch under colourful awnings. Fish is prepared simply or in more elaborate Sicilian dishes. ⊗ Via Cernia 13 • Map F6 • 0932 937 710 • Closed Mon in winter • €€€

9 La Cialoma, Marzamemi

Enthusiastic service, a tasty mainly fish-based menu and a great wine list are all on offer in this romantic square with live music in summer (see p77). ⊗ Piazza Regina Margherita 23 • Map G6 • 0931 841 772 • Closed Tue (Dec–May), Nov • €€€

10 La Darsena da Iannuzzo, Syracuse

Feast on fresh fish, perfectly and traditionally cooked, in the spacious dining room or the waterfront terrace, on the beautiful island of Ortygia. ⊗ Riva Garibaldi 6, Ortygia • Map H5 • 0931 61522 • Closed Mon • €€

Note: Unless otherwise stated, all restaurants accept credit cards and serve vegetarian meals.

STREETSMART

SICILY'S TOP 10

Left **Busy summer street scene** Centre **Tourist office sign** Right **Beach in summer**

General Information

1 When to Go
The best times to visit are May, June, September and October. Summer is lovely, but it can get very hot in July and August, and the beaches are crowded.

2 What to Pack
If you're heading for Etna or Stromboli, take hiking shoes, a torch and a warm coat; if it's a beach destination, you'll need a swimsuit, sandals for pebble beaches, sunglasses, sun protection and a beach towel.

3 Tourist Offices Abroad
Ente Nazionale Italiano per il Turismo is the national Italian tourist board and has offices in numerous countries. ⊗ www.enit.it
• USA: 630 Fifth Ave, Suite 1965, New York, NY 10111; (212) 245 5618
• UK: 1 Princes St, London W1B 2AY; (020) 7408 1254

4 Tourist Offices in Sicily
Tourist offices in Sicily usually have information on local attractions and events such as concerts and exhibitions, as well as hotel and restaurant listings. Look for signs with an "i", usually on a yellow or blue background.

5 Embassies and Consulates
British consulates are in Palermo and Catania, and there is a US Consular Agency in Palermo.

⊗ British Embassy in Rome: 039 06 4220 0001
• Emergency consular assistance (24 hours): 44 (0) 207 008 1500; www.embassypages.com • US Consular Agency: Via Vaccarini 1, Palermo; 091 305 857; www.usembassy.it

6 Passports and Visas
Non-EU citizens need a valid passport to enter Italy; EU members can use an identity card or passport. Visas are not required for citizens of the EU, USA, Canada, Australia or New Zealand for stays of less than three months. Other nationalities should check with their embassies. Apply for visas in person and well in advance at the Italian embassy or consular office in your home country.

7 Customs
EU residents are not charged duty on goods purchased in Italy, although certain limits may apply. US citizens are allowed to bring in up to $800 worth of goods. No fruits, vegetables, meats, cheeses or farm products can be brought in.

8 Public Holidays
Shops, post offices and banks close on public holidays (see box).

9 Electricity and Water
Electrical current is 220V, and plugs have two or three round prongs. Sicily is notorious for poor water supplies – periods of drought are frequent. Small inland towns have the most problems, but hotels are well equipped. Everyone drinks bottled water, although tap water is usually potable.

10 Opening Hours
Shops open between 8:30am and 10am; food shops often open earlier. Most shops close for a few hours at lunchtime, then stay open until 8pm.

Public Holidays

New Year's Day
1 Jan

Epiphany
6 Jan

Easter Monday

Liberation Day
25 Apr

Labour Day
1 May

Republic Day
2 Jun

Ferragosto
15 Aug

All Saints' Day
1 Nov

Immaculate Conception
8 Dec

Christmas Day
25 Dec

Santo Stefano
26 Dec

Whether you are hiking or spending a day at the beach, it's always advisable to carry a bottle of water.

Left **Fontanarossa Airport, Catania** Right **Punta Raisi Airport, Palermo**

Getting to Sicily

1 By Air from Europe
British Airways, Air Malta and Ryanair fly direct from London year-round. Some other carriers provide direct flights to Sicily in the summer. There are always numerous flights to Sicily from various airports in mainland Italy.

2 By Air from the Americas
There are no direct flights into Sicily from American airports. Flights from the Americas to Italy usually land in Milan or Rome, where connections can be made to Sicily.

3 By Air from Australia
There are no direct flights to Sicily. Fly into a major Italian airport such as Milan or Rome and make a connection to one of the Sicilian airports. It is usually cheaper to fly to London and catch a low-cost flight from there.

4 Palermo Airport, Punta Raisi
Palermo airport lies west of the city, about 40 minutes from the centre and an hour or so from Trapani. The Prestia e Comandè bus service runs between Punta Raisi and Palermo every half-hour, with various stops, including the port and the main train station. There is also a train service, the Trinacria Express.
◆ www.aeroporto.palermo.it

5 Catania Airport, Fontanarossa
Convenient for the eastern side of the island and just 20 minutes from Catania's centre, Fontanarossa Airport has been modernized with new terminal buildings. The airport buses (Alibus) leave every 20 minutes between 5am and midnight, stopping at the airport, Via Etnea and the central train station.
◆ www.aeroporto.catania.it

6 Other Airports
Located at Birgi, in the northwest, Trapani is a Ryanair hub in Sicily. It's a good alternative to Palermo's Punta Raisi airport. Ryanair now also flies into Comiso, in the southeast of the island, close to Ragusa ◆ www.airgest.it; www.aeroportodicomiso.com

7 Domestic Airports
While Palermo, Catania, Comiso and Trapani airports handle international flights, the smaller airports of Pantelleria and Lampedusa are limited to domestic flights.

8 By Train
Trains from mainland Italy are loaded onto boats and ferried across the straits of Messina, calling at Messina before making their way south to Catania or west to Palermo. Check with your travel agent for times and fares or directly with the Italian State Railway. ◆ Italian State Railway: Ferrovie dello Stato; 89 20 21; www.trenitalia.it

9 By Car
If you want to travel in your own car rather than renting one on the island, you can take a traghetto (ferry) to Sicily from Genoa, Livorno, Naples or Reggio di Calabria. From Reggio or nearby San Giovanni, take FS, Caronte or Meridiano across the Straits of Messina to Messina itself (30 mins). Grandi Navi Veloci takes 20 hours from Genoa to Palermo or 18 hours from Livorno to Palermo. Tirrenia sails from Naples to Palermo in 16 hours. Siremar sails from Naples to the Aeolian Islands and Milazzo in 11 hours. ◆ Tirrenia: Naples: 081 0171 998 (892 123 in Italy); www.Tirrenia.it • SNAV: 081 428 5555; www.snav.it • Grandi Navi Veloci: 010 209 4591; www.gnv.it • Siremar: 023 959 5015 (199 118 866 in Italy); www.siremar.it

10 By Boat
Ferry details for foot passengers are as above, but if you are on foot you can also take a faster aliscafo (hydrofoil), with services offered by Siremar, SNAV (see above) and Ustica Lines. ◆ Ustica Lines: 0923 873 813; www.usticalines.it

Left **City bus transport** Right **Travelling by scooter**

Getting Around Sicily

1 By Car
It is easiest to get around Sicily by car, particularly in the remote interior. Bring a good map, an international driving licence, and all the necessary paperwork for your vehicle, since documents must be presented during spot checks. Beware of city traffic: the fast-moving pace, impatient Italian drivers and narrow, one-way streets can be nerve-racking. In Palermo and Catania, it is best to park the car and explore by bus and on foot. ✆ Roadside assistance: 116.

2 Car Rental
Car-rental agencies can be found at major airports and in cities and larger towns. Most companies do not charge a drop-off fee if you remain on the island, so you can pick a car up in Palermo and drop it off in Catania, for example, for no extra charge.

3 Road Rules
Sicily's reputation for aggressive drivers may seem deserved at first glance but if you look closely, you'll notice that everybody lets everyone else cut in. Make eye contact, take advantage of an opening, and merge. There are, of course, people who just ignore all the rules, so always stay alert.

4 City Public Transport
Bus service in cities and large towns is reliable and extensive, and a good way to get around. Tickets are available from kiosks near major stops, from some bars and from tobacconists (look for the black sign with a "T"). Validate your ticket in the yellow machine once on board.

5 By Train
Train services, provided by the Italian State Railways (Ferrovie dello Stato) do exist in Sicily, but with more routes available in the eastern part of the island than in the west. Timetables are available on the Internet (see p129) or at train stations. The service is mostly reliable. Before travelling, validate your ticket in one of the yellow machines on the platform.

6 By Bus
Bus services are comprehensive and used a lot by Sicilians, who often work or attend school or university away from their home village. A variety of regional bus companies provide coverage throughout the island (reduced service on Sundays and holidays). The main bus companies are SAIS, Interbus, Etna Transporti and AST. Bus stations are called auto-stazione, and are usually located near train stations.

7 By Bicycle
If you are an experienced cyclist, Sicily offers some good biking opportunities but beware of the long distances and steep inclines. Bicycles are for rent in cities and on the offshore islands, at very reasonable rates.

8 By Boat
Ferries (traghetti) and hydrofoils (aliscafi) ply the routes between Sicily and the offshore islands, ports on mainland Italy, as well as Sardinia and Corsica (see p129). Private boats, with a captain if you prefer, are available for rent from many ports, and fishermen quite often offer short trips in summer.

9 By Scooter
Scooter rentals are reasonably priced and a fun way to get around smaller towns and the offshore islands. Rental companies provide helmets, instructions and usually a map. It is not recommended for big city transport, as the traffic is chaotic and truly dangerous for scooters.

10 Taxi
Taxis are available in cities from marked taxi stands and work on a metered basis. Taxi drivers are also open to setting a fee for a day or more of a private service if you want to get around without driving yourself.

If driving in Sicily, watch out for stop signs that are often painted directly on the road rather than overhead on road signs.

Left **Escorted tour of Selinunte** Right **Horse riding in the Madonie mountains**

TOP 10 Specialist Holidays

1 Food Tours

The Slow Food movement began in Italy, promoting and protecting traditional farming and food production. It runs a range of gastronomic and cultural tours. Sicily-based Siqillhyàh offers visits to traditional farms, some offering rooms or cottages. Peggy Markel's Culinary Adventures has a food-orientated tour of Sicily. ✆ *Slow Food Travel: www. slowfoodtravel.it • Siqillhyàh: www.siqillyah.it • Peggy Markel's Culinary Adventures: www. peggymarkel.com*

2 Italian Language

Taormina's Babilonia language school holds courses for between five and ten people, at various levels. Solemar runs language courses in Aspra, near Palermo, and Cefalù, and Reusia Centrolingue runs courses in Ragusa. ✆ *Babilonia Centro di Lingua e Cultura Italiana: 0942 23 441; www.babilonia. it • Solemar: Aspra: 091 955 561, Cefalù: 0921 921 029; www.solemar-sicilia.it • Reusia: www.reusia.com*

3 Senior Citizen Holidays

The US-based company Road Scholar offers tours emphasizing art, history and archaeology for the over-55s. Their Sicily tours include a good range of sites. Lectures give an insight into the culture, with additional topics such as cuisine, literature and

the Mafia. ✆ *(800) 454 5768; www.roadscholar.org*

4 Art and Painting

Sicily's vivid colours and stunning land- and seascapes have long been an inspiration for artists. The UK-based company Art Holidays runs courses at the Fattoria Mosè farmhouse, near Agrigento *(see p143)*. ✆ *020 7609 0843 • www.art-holidays.com*

5 Hiking

Country Walkers offers hiking trips to Sicily, including the Aeolian Islands, with English-speaking guides. Ramblers Holidays offers tours that include Etna, the ancient wonders of Sicily, and a combined cruise and walking holiday. ✆ *Country Walkers (USA): 800 464 9255; www.countrywalkers.com • Ramblers Holidays (UK): 01707 331 133; www. ramblersholidays.com*

6 Tours and Activities

The Sicilian Experience has a range of tours of the island, as well as a variety of activity holidays, including sailing, scuba diving, walking and golf. ✆ *020 7828 9171; www.the sicilianexperience.co.uk*

7 Horse Riding

Castelbuono Trekking organizes holidays on horseback in the Madonie mountains, as well as individual excursions.

Many *agriturismi* offer horse riding. You can also contact local riding stables through the national park offices. ✆ *Castelbuono Trekking: 339 489 6332; www.castelbuonotrekking.it • Parco Regionale delle Madonie: 0921 684 011; www.parcodellemadonie.it • Parco Regionale dei Nebrodi: 199 11 22 00; www.parcodeinebrodi.it*

8 Cookery Courses

Renowned chef Valentina Harris runs a course from Fattoria Mosè *(see p143)*. The Love Sicily cookery school is based in Modica. ✆ *Valentina Harris (UK): 0781 806 4157; www. valentinaharris.com • Love Sicily: 020 8133 6251 (UK), 0932 950 222 (Italy); www. lovesicily.com*

9 Escorted Tours

Best of Sicily and Italia Tours run a range of escorted tours, many with a particular theme, such as food history or culture. They also offer one-day excursions. ✆ *Best of Sicily: www.best ofsicily.com • Italia Tours: www.italiatours.com*

10 Motorbike Tours

Motoexplora arranges motorbike tours that take in some of Sicily's major sights, as well as its hidden treasures. The routes follow the island's less frequented roads. You can even hire a bike if you don't want to bring your own. ✆ *095 765 26 13 • www.motoexplora.com*

Streetsmart

Discover more at www.traveldk.com

Left **Driving on a narrow Sicilian street** Right **Mountain snake**

🔟 Things to Avoid

Tourist Meals
A fixed-price meal can be a good deal, but avoid tourist meals offering generic Italian dishes such as *pasta alla bolognese* or *spaghetti alla carbonara*. Instead, seek out unpretentious *trattorie* frequented by locals. Here you will eat simple dishes prepared with high-quality and fresh Sicilian ingredients.

The Mafia
The Mafia does not bother tourists and it's highly unlikely that you would run into anything connected to the group. Sicilians are more comfortable now about speaking out against Mafia violence; however, although they are generous with advice and directions, they remain suspicious of anyone asking too many questions.

Snakes
Be on the lookout for snakes in the mountains or sunning themselves on the ancient stones of archaeological sites. For the most part they are not poisonous and slither off as soon as disturbed, but it's a good idea to wear shoes and socks instead of sandals when clambering around ruins.

Chemical Plants
Sadly, not all of Sicily's coastline is pristine. Particularly east of Palermo, near Milazzo, between Catania and Syracuse, and near Gela, there are enormous petrochemical plants, usually marked with signs saying *agglomerato industriale* and belching pollution into the air and sea water.

Large Cars
If you're driving, don't rent a car larger than you need. In big cities it will be hard to park, and in small towns and villages it will be hard to squeeze through narrow city gates or tiny streets designed to bear nothing wider than a mule-drawn cart. It helps to look ahead for vehicles to ensure the street is transitable – some village roads narrow until they become footpaths or become so steep they turn into staircases.

Dressing Inappropriately
Not every church enforces dress rules, but they can if they want to. Short skirts and shorts are not appreciated, and nor are skimpy tops with bare shoulders. Simply covering your shoulders with a scarf or a make-shift shawl usually solves the problem.

Backtracking
Sicily is deceptively large. Avoid backtracking over great distances to catch your flight home. Fly into one airport and out of another if touring.

Forest Fires
Lack of rain and the broiling sun make Sicily very dry in summer, and forest fires are common. Make sure you don't set them off by extinguishing cigarettes properly and not lighting campfires unless it is expressly allowed. If you see a fire, call the *Incendi Boschivi* (forest fire) hotline on 1515. If you are near a fire, try to stay up wind and follow the instructions of the *Vigili del Fuoco* (firemen).

Theft
You're no more prone to thieves in Sicily than anywhere else in Italy, but use general common sense. Lock your car, don't leave any items exposed (including the radio), keep an eye on your wallet and backpack in crowded places, don't flaunt jewellery, use caution at ATMs, and don't leave valuables unattended on the beach.

Scams
Market stalls putting on the hard sell don't always have the freshest goods. It is a good idea to compare prices at different stalls if you are suspicious of being ripped off. Beware also of the expensive *"giro d'isola"* tour of the island, offered by taxi services on the offshore islands. Make sure the meter is running or set your price in advance.

Left **Food products to take home** Right **Wine shop**

🔟 Shopping Tips

1 Opening Hours
Most shops are open 8:30 or 9am to 1pm and about 3:30 to 7:30 or 8pm, but times can vary. Shops are required to post their hours on the door. In tourist areas in summer shops stay open during lunch, as do many supermarkets and department stores in the larger cities. Many stores close for one half-day during the week, usually Monday mornings or Wednesday afternoons. Hairdressers and barbers are closed all day Monday.

2 How to Pay
Credit cards and traveller's cheques are not as widely accepted or appreciated as cash. You'll also get a discount for paying in cash on occasion (or pay slightly more for a credit card transaction).

3 Tax Refunds
Value added tax (IVA) is included in the price of goods for sale in stores. Non-EU citizens can get the tax refunded if they spend more than €155 in any one store. The procedure is relatively simple if the shop adheres to the Tax Free Shopping initiative – you simply get a refund at their office at the airport. If the shop is not part of the initiative, the bureaucracy is rather more complex – make sure you always ask for a *fattura*, or invoice.

4 Ceramics
Artisan ceramic production in Sicily is of good quality. Traditional styles vary from area to area and some craftsmen produce good modern designs as well. Examine each piece carefully to make sure there are no gaps in the glaze. You might be able to bargain for a discount on a slightly flawed piece. If you want the ceramics posted home, most stores are adept at packing and shipping, but make sure insurance is included or they have an arrangement with their courier service.

5 Haggling
Haggling is common in markets for any items except food, which is so reasonably priced that you won't need to haggle anyway. Shops do not haggle over prices unless something is flawed. But if you spend a lot in a particular store, it never hurts to ask for a *sconto* (discount).

6 Puppets
Tourist shops are full of puppets, varying in quality. Some craftsmen who produce puppets for performances also make puppets for sale as souvenirs, usually slightly smaller in scale than those used in the theatre. Antiques shops sell puppets too, but if it's the real item expect to pay a high price.

7 Wine
Numerous Sicilian wines are currently among the most popular and widely respected, both on the Italian market and further afield *(see pp72–3)*. Larger shops and vineyards will ship wines home for you.

8 Food
Unperishable food products allow you to bring a bit of Sicily home. Most shops offer canned goods or items shrink-wrapped *(sotto vuoto)*. Look for olive oils and anything preserved in salt or oil, such as tuna, sundried tomatoes, olives, capers and artichokes. There are good Sicilian cookbooks in English – look for those written by Anna Tasca Lanza and Mary Taylor Simeti.

9 Fabric Items
Erice is well known for the *frazzata*, a brightly coloured woven rug. On the east of the island, around Ragusa, Syracuse and Catania, embroidered shawls and other items are made using the traditional *sfilato* method.

10 Terracotta
Hand-moulded terracotta figurines have long played a part in the Nativity scene tradition, representing folks from all walks of life. You can find old figurines in antiques shops; some craftsmen still make them using traditional methods.

If buying Sicilian wine to take home, check the regulations for shipping alcohol into your home country.

Left **Lifeguard patrol** Right **Beachside bar**

🔟 Tips for Families

1 Attitude To Kids

Sicilians love children. Restaurants, bars, and hotels are eager to accommodate families and children, so there is no need to be shy about asking for special favours or services.

2 Accommodation

Resort villages have staff on hand to take care of children and entertain them with supervised group activities. Call ahead to find out the age groups provided for and the kinds of services and activities on offer.

3 Meals

Restaurant menus do not usually have a separate section for children, but a *mezza porzione* (half-portion) is usually available on request. For simple, non-spicy dishes, ask for *pasta al pomodoro* (with tomatoes) or *pasta/riso in bianco* (pasta or rice with olive oil). Highchairs are often available.

4 Water Safety

Only the larger and more populated beaches have *bagnini* (lifeguards), and, if they do, there should be a red flag flying when they aren't on duty or when the sea is considered rough or unsafe for swimming. Trained as the lifeguards may be, it's always a

good idea to keep an eye on your kids yourself. The *alimentari* and souvenir shops that abound in most seaside villages sell all sorts of gear, from flippers and snorkels to armbands and sun protection.

5 Bathing

Almost every beach has at least one establishment that rents beach equipment for beachgoers, including umbrellas, chairs and pedal boats. The larger establishments have convenient showers and changing rooms, as well as a restaurant and a bar.

6 Extra Beds

It is usually possible to add an extra bed or cot to a double hotel room for a 30 per cent surcharge. Many hotels, of all categories, expect families and have rooms outfitted with three, four or five beds as a matter of course, as well as extra space.

7 Going Out

Sicilian families stick together and often eat out in large groups, socializing in the piazza or enjoying a *passeggiata* (see p52) until the early hours of the morning. As the summer drags on, the siesta gets longer and longer, meals start later and later, and local kids stay up until well after midnight.

8 Siesta

Take advantage of the afternoon siesta time to let children have a nap. It's not a bad idea for the parents, either! Most of Sicily shuts down during the hottest hours of the day (between noon and 4pm), and comes to life again when the air cools off in the evening.

9 Illness

If you haven't brought the medicines you need with you, feel under the weather or need any medical advice while in Sicily, start with a visit to a pharmacy. Italian pharmacists are trained to diagnose and treat minor problems and can recommend paediatricians. Holiday villages and campsites have seasonal infirmaries and your consular agent should be able to provide a list of paediatricians who speak your language (see p128). Most resorts and small islands also have a duty doctor (*guardia medica*).

10 Safety

Check in advance with your car rental company or travel agency that child car seats are available. If they are not, bring your own from home or hunt around for a company that includes them. Make sure that the rear seatbelts are in full working order before you set off.

Left **Eating at the bar** Right **Wholesale fish market**

Sicily on a Budget

1 Travel Discounts
Booking online often gets good deals with low-cost airlines. All-inclusive packages, including air or boat fare, food, lodging and sometimes car hire for one set price, can be a bargain, but they are generally only available during the summer season. Avoiding weekend travel usually means paying less.

2 Discounts
At the majority of sights and museums, there are reductions for groups and students under 25, and free entry for those under 12 and over 65 (sometimes this applies to EU citizens only). During European Heritage Days in September, and Italian Culture Week in April, there is free entry to many sights, including some not usually open to the public.

3 Accommodation
Hostels and *pensioni*, particularly those run by religious orders *(see p145)*, offer inexpensive, safe and clean lodging. Orange Juice is an association of 12 excellent B&Bs in great locations around Sicily. Providing itineraries and even arranging car hire, if required, they offer special prices for DIY tours that include a night or two in a variety of places.
◈ *Orange Juice: 0922 919 670; www.orangejuice.it*

4 Restaurants
Unassuming *trattorie* serve up hearty helpings of traditional foods – a crowd of locals is a good sign of the quality. House wine costs less than the listed wines; meat costs less than fish. Unless you're famished, a pasta dish and a *contorno*, or side dish, should be plenty, and is more affordable *(see p138)*.

5 Picnics
Scenic picnics are highly recommended and fit for any budget. *Alimentari* offer fresh, local salami, cheese and olives. Markets sell fresh fruits and vegetables, and bakeries and *alimentari* will often make sandwiches to order. Wine is available at reasonable prices.

6 Bars and Rosticcerie
Sicily has a long, rich tradition of fast, filling food in bars and *rosticcerie*. Look for *panelle*, *arancini*, *sfincione* and pizza, and enjoy the variety of pastries and sandwiches. It is cheaper to eat at the counter than to sit if there is table service.

7 Low Season
Hotels drop their prices considerably (as much as 40 per cent) out of the high season (July and August). The weather is nice and the water is good for swimming in

June and September. For discounts in the high season, when people hit the coast, look to cities and towns. Some hotels lure people inland with cheap rates in the summer.

8 Public Transport
Take advantage of buses, and ask about special day passes. Tickets are sold at the bus station in large towns, at kiosks near bus stops, at *tabacchi* (look for the black-and-white "T" sign) and in some bars, and must be validated upon entry in the bus. Do not throw tickets away, as you may be asked to prove you used them. Free bicycle rentals may be arranged at the tourist office in many areas.

9 Free Sites
Sicily is a living monument. The landscape, the sea, the lively markets and festivals, and the historic churches are among the finest things Sicily has to offer, and they are all free.

10 Museum Fees
A *biglietto cumulativo* (cumulative ticket) is a great way to save money. It's a one-price entry to several sights in the same area. However, you will have to request one, since the cashier at the ticket booth will not always offer you one automatically.

Left **Bancomat ATM sign** Right **Automatic exchange machine**

🔟 Banking and Communications

1 Currency
Along with many other countries in the European Union, Italy uses the euro as its common currency. Check newspapers and currency services for up-to-date exchange rates.

2 Changing Money
You can change money at banks and larger post offices wherever you go, and at *bureaux de change* and automatic exchange machines at airports and in the larger cities. Exchange rates and fees vary considerably, but post offices generally charge the lowest commission.

3 ATMs
Most banks have ATMs *(Bancomat)*, and you can find them all over Sicily, apart from remoter villages. Except for brief interruptions in service, they work 24 hours a day. The Italian banks don't usually charge a fee for using an ATM at their end, but your bank at home might charge a percentage of the transaction. Banks are most likely to charge a lower fee than a credit card company, whose fees for cash advances can be steep.

4 Credit cards
Credit cards are not always accepted. Be sure to ask first, or look for the credit card symbol on the window of a shop or restaurant. Plan to pay for a good portion of your trip in cash, especially for petrol. When credit cards are accepted, Visa, Master-Card and American Express are the most commonly used.

5 Traveller's Cheques
Traveller's cheques can be changed at hotels, banks and *bureaux de change*; however, be aware that the rates for foreign exchange are not usually good.

6 Telephones
Public telephones can be found in city streets and some bars. They operate with phone-cards purchased from *tabacchi* (tobacconists). The larger cities have a growing number of international telephone centres that offer competitive rates. In small villages, ask for *un telefono pubblico*. European mobile phones will have coverage, except in very mountainous areas. It is possible to buy a SIM card with an Italian number for about €10.

7 Internet
There are increasing numbers of Internet connection points on the island, usually in the cities and tourist areas. Anti-terrorist laws require that you present your passport and a photocopy of it when you register. Hotels often have an Internet point for guests. Big cities, such as Palermo and Catania, have Wi-Fi hot spots in public areas.

8 Post
Italian post offices function like banks, and there are often long, slow-moving queues. As with almost everything else, they generally close at lunchtime; many branches do not open in the afternoon. If you just need to purchase *francobolli* (stamps), save yourself the hassle and buy them from *tabacchi*.

9 Newspapers
US, British, French and German newspapers are available on newsstands in Palermo, Trapani, Catania and Messina. In the smaller villages and hinterlands, only tourist spots such as Taormina, the Aeolian Islands and Erice are likely to have any foreign newspapers on sale.

10 Television and Radio
Italian television is notoriously monotonous and often sexist. The better hotels will have satellite television broadcasting foreign channels such as the BBC, CNN or SkyNews. Radio coverage can be unreliable in the region's mountainous zones.

Left **Police car** Right **Sicilian pharmacy**

🔟 Security and Health

1 Emergency Numbers

The emergency telephone numbers for Italy's two main police forces are 112 for *carabinieri* and 113 for *polizia*. Dial 118 for an ambulance or a medical emergency, 115 to report a fire and 1515 for a forest fire.

2 Police

Carabinieri and *polizia* are both responsible for general security in Italy. The *carabinieri* (dark-blue uniforms with a red stripe) have a military background, while the *polizia* (pale-blue uniforms) are the state police. Thefts and other crimes can be reported to either – you should go to the *caserma dei carabinieri* (barracks) or to the *questura* (police station).

3 Health Insurance

EU citizens should get a European Health Insurance Card, which entitles them to emergency medical treatment. Citizens from elsewhere must have medical insurance that covers Italy. Usually, you pay hospital fees upfront and then apply for reimbursement.

4 Pharmacies

Pharmacists are trained to diagnose and treat minor problems. Many items for sale, regardless of whether or not a doctor's prescription is required, are kept behind the counter, so you usually have to ask for what you're looking for. Pointing to your sore throat is enough to let them know that you need lozenges, for example. A green cross signifies a pharmacy; if it's closed, there should be an indication of the nearest one that's open posted on or near the door. Toiletries are also available in *profumerie*.

5 Hospitals

If you are in need of medical assistance in an emergency, visit the casualty department *(pronto soccorso)* at the nearest hospital. In the remote interior, on the minor islands and at some resorts, go to the *guardia medica* (duty doctor) or, if necessary, dial the emergency number.

6 Dentists

Dental care is not covered by most travel insurance policies. If you have a problem that needs immediate attention, ask the local pharmacist to recommend a dentist, check with your consulate for a list of dentists who speak your language or, in an emergency, go to the nearest hospital's casualty department.

7 Theft

Although crime is not rampant, be aware of thieves, especially in crowded streets and markets. Report an incident to the police immediately. You may need documentation from the police to show to your insurance company.

8 Coastguards

The *guardia costiera* patrol all of Italy's coastline. Among their other duties, they are responsible for controlling pleasure craft. Boats registered in a country within the EU are not subject to customs control, but must have on board all papers necessary for the countries where the boat and skipper are registered, and must follow laws pertaining to Italian waters. For an emergency at sea, call the coastguard emergency number, 1530.

9 Fire

Wild fires break out easily in the dry summer and spread rapidly by the hot scirocco wind. Call the Vigili del Fuoco at 115 and 1515 for forest fires.

10 Water safety

Bagnini (lifeguards) are not always on duty at pools or beaches. There is no widespread use of the flag system, or wind and current signals. Although Sicily's waters are not particularly hazardous, it's a good idea to consider all swimming as "at your own risk". Call the coastguard (1530) in an emergency.

Left **Open-air** *trattoria* Right **Antipasto**

🔟 Dining Out Tips

1 Restaurant Types
Restaurants vary from the inexpensive *tavola calda*, serving hot and cold buffet platters, to casual *pizzerie*, *osterie* and *trattorie*, to the more elegant *ristorante*. An enjoyable meal is an important part of Italian life, so feel free to linger in any establishment as long as you like.

2 Breakfast
Hotels serve good strong coffee and bread, if not a full buffet. Out and about, bars serve strong *espresso*, or *cappuccino* early in the day, usually accompanied by a *cornetto* (croissant) or *arancini (see p71)*.

3 Antipasto
Antipasto literally means "before the meal". It can be anything from salami and cheese, to marinated anchovies, or any creative little bite the chef has prepared.

4 Primo
This is the first course, and is usually a soup, pasta or rice cooked with vegetables, and some fish or meat. You can ask for a *mezza porzione* if you don't want a full plate of pasta, but be prepared to pay the full price for it anyway in some places. If you order couscous with fish (a Sicilian speciality), it's often served as a *piatto unico* (single course), since it

includes both ingredients on the same plate.

5 Secondo
Second courses are based on meat or fish. A selection of grilled meats and *involtini* (slices of meat rolled around a stuffing) are usually on offer. Excellent fresh fish is available in almost every eatery on the island. The *secondo* is usually served alone on the plate; however, it is perfectly acceptable to eat the course accompanied by bread and vegetables or salad.

6 Contorni
Contorni are vegetable side dishes that accompany the *secondo*. They usually consist of salads, tomato salad, grilled vegetables or roasted potatoes, French fries or greens.

7 Cheese, Desserts and Coffee
After the main meal, you might be offered the *formaggio* (cheese) course. Ask for the speciality of the area. Fruit is almost always available and may accompany the cheese. *Dolci* (desserts) in Sicily *(see p71)* are excellent and often made in-house. Finally, coffee is served at the end of every meal. If it's late and you'd prefer to avoid the caffeine, ask for your coffee to be *decaffeinato* (decaffeinated).

8 Tipping
Bills for meals include *il coperto* (a small cover charge) and sometimes a *servizio* (service charge) of around 10 per cent, which will be marked on the bill. If service charges are not included, you aren't usually expected to leave a tip, although it's always a nice gesture. An Italian will usually leave a few euros in a *trattoria* if the service and food were good, or if it's a place they frequent regularly. They leave a little more in a restaurant.

9 Wine
You'll be offered the house wine in a half- or full-litre carafe. If you are at all interested in wines, take a look at the wine list, as there are usually at least a few good bottles at decent prices. Try a *malvasia*, *passito* or Marsala with cheese or dessert, or as an after-dinner drink.

10 Bars
All Sicilian bars serve coffee, pastries and sandwiches, specialities such as *arancini*, as well as beer, wine, *spumante* (sparkling wine) and a range of other alcoholic beverages. They are open from early in the morning until late at night. As a rule of thumb, it is always more expensive to eat or drink seated at a table than it is to stand at the bar.

Look out for the snail sticker, which indicates the restaurant belongs to the "Slow Food" movement (the opposite of fast food).

Left & Right **Typical Sicilian hotels**

TOP 10 Accommodation Tips

1 Hotels
There are now many top-quality hotels and bed-and-breakfast establishments throughout Sicily. The choice of places to stay is wider in popular destinations such as Taormina and the larger cities, while hotels are still rather more thin on the ground in Sicily's inland areas.

2 Grading
Hotels are graded according to a star system, from one to five. One-star hotels are inexpensive and offer a choice of rooms with or without bath. Two- and three-star hotels are functional and are usually clean. Most four-star hotels have added comforts such as swimming pools and modern bathrooms. The island's few five-star hotels are luxurious.

3 Reservations
Always book in advance in high season (July and August), but outside of these months you can usually book just a day or two ahead. Many places accept bookings via email; if not, telephone or send a fax. A deposit is sometimes required to confirm a booking. The staff at hotel reception desks usually speak enough foreign languages to make and confirm reservations.

4 High and Low Season
High season is July and August and most room rates go up during that time. Expect to pay more for rooms on the off-shore islands and at popular resorts such as Taormina. Some hotels also require a *mezza pensione* (half-board) deal during high season. Prices drop as much as 40 per cent outside of high season.

5 Villas
Various foreign and local companies offer homes for rent, from countryside villas and seaside homes to apartments in a city or town. For a small group or family, renting a house can be economical, but make sure you check the insurance cover carefully.

6 Farms
There has been an explosion of agritourism in the last few years in Sicily and there is a wide range of quality and services. Some offer tranquil private accommodation or apartment rentals on small farms; others have the option to get involved in activities, such as picking grapes.
- www.agriturist.it
- www.turismoverde.it
- www.agriturismosicilia.it

7 Camping
There are plenty of campsites along Sicily's coastline and a few inland, rated with a star system like hotels and usually well equipped with swimming pools, *pizzerias*, bars, beach facilities, and sometimes an infirmary in summer. Pitching a tent outside of official campsites is not allowed.
- www.camping.it
- www.campeggi.com

8 Half Board
In high season some agritourism and resort hotels require that you take half board, which means breakfast and one other meal included in the price of your room. Some offer *pensione completa* (full board).

9 Private Rooms
Private rooms for rent are available in most tourist areas, particularly the offshore islands, at Cefalù and Taormina. You'll usually have more than your fair share to choose from disembarking from a hydrofoil or in train stations. Tourist offices and travel agencies also have listings.

10 Hostels
Much cheaper than traditional hotel rooms, hostels often have private rooms as well as dormitories. They also provide local information, laundry and kitchen facilities, television and Internet access. Some have bars and offer room rates with breakfast or other meals.

For specialist Sicilian dishes **See pp70–71**
For accommodation in Sicily **See pp140–47**

Left **Eremo della Giubiliana** Right **Grand Hotel Villa Igiea**

TOP 10 Luxury Hotels

1 Eremo della Giubiliana, Ragusa

This elegant 15th-century monastic building has just 13 rooms, six suites and five cottages, meaning that each guest is treated to the most attentive service. Rooms, public areas and grounds are authentically restored with wood and iron furnishings, fountains and stone courts. Excellent restaurant and garden with pool. ✆ *Contrada Giubiliana • Map F5 • 0932 669 119 • Dis. access • www.eremodella giubiliana.it • €€€€€*

2 Grand Hotel Baia Verde, Catania

The 147 rooms and 10 suites, all newly renovated and with living area and a terrace, surround the palm-planted pool area and look out to the Ionian Sea. ✆ *Via Angelo Musco 8, Cannizzaro • Map G4 • 095 491 522 • www. baiaverde.it • €€€*

3 Grand Hotel Timeo & Villa Flora, Taormina

The Timeo is nestled into the bougainvillea- and palm-covered hillside just beneath Taormina's ancient Greek Theatre. The 70 rooms are in grand Baroque style. The bar and restaurant occupy terraces with amazing views. ✆ *Via Teatro Greco 59 • Map H3 • 0942 23 801 • www.belmond.com/it/ grand-hote-timeo-taormina • €€€€€*

4 San Domenico Palace, Taormina

Built as a monastery in the 1400s, it now houses 105 rooms and offers views of the bay and Mount Etna, a fitness room, beauty corner, pool and gym. ✆ *Piazza San Domenico 5 • Map H3 • 0942 613 111 • Dis. access • www.san-domenico-palace.comt • €€€€€*

5 Grand Hotel Villa Igiea, Palermo

Art Nouveau master Ernesto Basile built this grand villa at the end of the 19th century on the slopes of Monte Pellegrino. Dine on the terraces overlooking the sea. ✆ *Salita Belmonte 43 • Map L2 • 091 631 21 11 • Dis. access • www. hotelvilla-igiea.com • €€€€€*

6 Hotel Palazzo Failla, Modica

Most rooms in this conservatively restored antique *palazzo* retain their original patrician furnishings and colourful majolica floors. The ground floor is home to an elegant bar and La Gazza Ladra *(see p125)*, one of Sicily's best restaurants. ✆ *Via Blandini 5 • Map G6 • 0932 941 059 • www. palazzofailla.it • €€*

7 Villa Angela, Taormina

Rocker Jim Kerr has put together a comfortable yet hip resort hotel. Perched above Taormina, it has views over the town and out to the sea. Staff arrange activities, beach access and excursions. ✆ *Via Leonardo da Vinci • Map H3 • 0942 270 38 • www. hotelvillaangela.com • €€€€€*

8 Terre di Vendicari, Noto

Just four rooms in luxuriously renovated farm buildings, attentive service and calming hues of white and ochre. Nestle into one of the four-poster beds on the terrace and follow the line of the swimming pool out to the sea on the horizon. ✆ *Contrada Vaddeddi • Map G6 • 346 359 38 45 • www. terredivendicari.it • €€€€€*

9 Excelsior Palace Hotel, Taormina

This four-star hotel is notable for the views of Etna and for the gardens with swimming pool on a promontory overlooking the Bay of Naxos. ✆ *Via Toselli 8 • Map H3 • 0942 239 75 • www.excelsior palacetaormina.it • €€€€€*

10 Locanda Don Serafino, Ragusa Ibla

Many of this hotel's 10 rooms are carved out of the rocky cliffside to which Ibla clings. The hotel offers distinctive rooms and chic add-ons: a Michelin-starred restaurant, a private lido at Marina di Ragusa, and a seaside pizzeria. ✆ *Via XI Febbraio 15 • Map F5 • 0932 220 065 • www. locandadonserafino.it • €€€*

Note: *Unless otherwise stated, all hotels accept credit cards, and have en-suite bathrooms and air conditioning.*

Price Categories

For a standard, double room per night (with breakfast if included), taxes and extra charges.

€	under €50
€€	€50–€100
€€€	€100–€150
€€€€	€150–€200
€€€€€	over €200

Above **Foresteria Baglio della Luna**

🔟 Historic Hotels

1 Foresteria Baglio della Luna, Agrigento

Guests are made to feel at home in this restored 13th-century tower and 18th-century *baglio*. The bright, intimate, central courtyard leads onto terraces shaded by olive and fruit trees with views to Agrigento's famed temples *(see pp26–9)*. Rooms on the upper level are furnished with antiques. ◊ *Via S A Guastella 1, Valle de' Templi • Map D4 • 0922 511 061 • www.bagliodellaluna.com • €€€€*

2 Hotel Relais Modica

This renovated *palazzo* opened in 2002. There are lovely views of Modica, a terrace and family rooms. The service is friendly. ◊ *Via Tommaso Campailla 99 • Map G6 • 0932 754 451 • www. hotelrelaismodica.it • €€*

3 Hotel Belvedere, Taormina

Built as a grand hotel in 1902 on Taormina's hillside, renovations have preserved the charm of the original while modernizing the guest rooms (most of them have good views). The Belvedere is also noted for its gardens with citrus and palm trees and serves poolside lunches. ◊ *Via Bagnoli Croci 79 • Map H3 • 0942 23 791 • www.villabelvedere.it • €€€€*

4 Hotel L'Ariana, Rinella, Salina

This whimsical turn-of-the-20th-century villa built onto the rocks above the tiny port of Rinella has been in the same family since shortly after it was built. Rooms are simple, and the best ones are those on the first floor, which open onto an ample terrace with amazing views. ◊ *Via Rotabile 11 • Map G1 • 090 980 90 75 • www. hotelariana.it • €€€€€*

5 Il Principe Hotel, Catania

This carefully renovated Baroque-style building is set in the historic heart of Catania. Rooms offer every modern comfort and, for additional luxury, do try the Turkish bath. ◊ *Via Alessi 20/26i • Map G4 • 0952 500 345 • www. ilprincipehotel.com • €€€€*

6 Atelier sul Mare, Castel di Tusa

It's not the building that is historic here, but the rooms themselves. Each room is an installation piece created by a modern artist, with evolving designs that guests are asked to participate in. Each room has a seafront terrace. Within easy reach of Cefalù, the Madonie mountains and the Fiumara d'Arte sculpture garden. ◊ *Via Cesare Battisti 4 • Map E2 • 0921 334 295 • www.atelier sulmare.it • €€€*

7 Palazzo Conte Federico, Palermo

This Norman palace is located in the heart of the old city, close to all monuments and a market. Apartments, some with private entrance, retain their original, imposing medieval furnishings. ◊ *Via dei Biscottari 4 • Map K5 • 091 651 18 81 • www. contefederico.com • €€€€*

8 Baglio Spanò, Petrosino, near Marsala

This gorgeous country house set in citrus groves and dating from the 1800s has six traditionally decorated rooms and a restaurant serving excellent food. ◊ *Contrada Triglia Scaletta • Map B3 • 348 882 20 95 • www.bagliospano.com • €€€*

9 Massimo Plaza, Palermo

In this renovated *palazzo*, rooms are soundproofed and take in views of the piazza. The stairs are very steep, and there is no lift. Parking. ◊ *Via Maqueda 437 • Map L4 • 091 325 657 • www.massimo plazahotel.com • €€*

10 Grand Hotel et des Palmes, Palermo

This hotel was built in the mid-1800s and later converted to Art Nouveau style. There are columned and marble public spaces and a gym. ◊ *Via Roma 398 • Map L3 • 091 602 81 11 • Dis. access • www. hotel-despalmes.it • €€€*

Left **Hotel del Corso** Right **Centrale Palace Hotel**

TOP10 Comfortable Hotels

1 Centrale Palace Hotel, Palermo

An elegant, restored *palazzo* with luxurious marble-clad public areas. Guests can enjoy romantic dinners and splendid views on the roof terrace. ◐ *Corso Vittorio Emanuele 327 • Map L5 • 091 336 666 • Dis. access • www. centralepalacehotel.com • €€€*

2 Hotel Pomara, San Michele di Ganzaria

The Pomara is one of the most comfortable options inland. The location is rustic and affords excellent views of the rolling, wheat-covered hills, but the hotel itself is modern. Great views from the pool, excellent restaurant on site, and convenient for visiting Enna, Piazza Armerina, Morgantina and Caltagirone. ◐ *Via Vittorio Veneto 84 • Map F4 • 0933 976 976 • Dis. access • www.hotel pomara.com • €€*

3 Hotel Posta, Palermo

This three-star hotel is an excellent bargain choice in Palermo. The 27 rooms are large and clean, the public areas are equipped with a TV, and parking is available. The Hotel Posta is situated near the church of San Domenico. ◐ *Via Gagini 77 • Map L3 • 091 587 338 • www.hotel postapalermo.it • €€€*

4 Katane Palace, Catania

This modern hotel has 60 spacious rooms in a renovated *palazzo* just steps from one of the city's daily markets and the chic Via Etnea. Helpful staff, elegant bar and on-site restaurant. Parking is also available, but book in advance. ◐ *Via Finocchiaro Aprile 110 • Map G4 • 095 747 07 02 • www.katanepalace.it • €€€*

5 Hotel del Corso, Taormina

A family-run, three-star hotel recommended by locals, with good views. The modern rooms have small terraces looking over the hillside, the Bay of Naxos and Mount Etna. Parking is available. ◐ *Corso Umberto I, 238 • Map H3 • 0942 628 698 • www.hoteldelcorso taormina.com • €€€*

6 Nuovo Hotel Russo, Trapani

Part of the Sole hotel chain, in an excellent location in Trapani's historic centre. The hotel resembles a grandmother's living room despite a makeover. Rooms are serviceable and clean. Reserve a parking space in their tiny garage for a small fee. They usually encourage you to go out for breakfast, which is a joy in lively Trapani. ◐ *Via Tintori 4 • Map B2 • 0923 22 163 • €€*

7 Hotel Gutkowski, Syracuse

In summer, breakfast is served on the terrace at this hotel on the Ortygia seafront. Guests can enjoy a drink at the hotel's own wine bar. ◐ *Lungomare Vittorini 26 • Map H5 • 0931 465 861 • Dis. access • www.guthotel.it • €€€*

8 Hotel Il Barocco, Ragusa Ibla

Rooms are comfortable at this centrally located hotel, the staff are helpful, parking is available and there is a breakfast room on site. A great base for exploring southeast Sicily. ◐ *Via Santissima Maria La Nuova 5 • Map F5 • 0932 663 105 • www.ilbarocco.it • €€€*

9 Albergo Aegusa, Favignana

Modern rooms, a terrace and a small garden restaurant, all tucked away in Favignana town. ◐ *Via Garibaldi 11 • Map A3 • 0923 922 430 • Dis. access • www.aegusahotel.it • €€€€*

10 Relais Antiche Saline, Paceco

This renovated historic building has spacious rooms with views over the Egadi Islands and the saltpans of Trapani's coast. There are also a pool area and a restaurant. Transport to Trapani upon request. ◐ *Via Verdi, Località Nubia • Map B2 • 0923 868 042 • www.relaisantiche saline.com • €€€€*

 Note: *Unless otherwise stated, all hotels accept credit cards, and have en-suite bathrooms and air conditioning.*

Price Categories

For a standard, double room per night (with breakfast if included), taxes and extra charges.

€	under €50
€€	€50–€100
€€€	€100–€150
€€€€	€150–€200
€€€€€	over €200

Above **Locanda COS**

Agriturismo and B&Bs

1 Rosemarie Tasca d'Almerita's, Vallelunga

Rosemarie Tasca d'Almerita opens her home on the family's Regaleali wine estate as a B&B. Relax on her rose-planted terraces, walk through the vineyards and tour the winery. There are three bedrooms, two with private baths; and dinner and lunch are optional. ⊗ *Tenuta Regaleali, Via Nazionale 108* • *Map E3* • *0921 544 032* • *No credit cards* • *www.sicilyathome.it* • *€€€*

2 Tenuta Gangivecchio

The estate deep in the Madonie mountains was founded as an abbey in 1363 but has been in the Tornabene family since 1856. Stay in a private cottage or one of eight rooms in the converted stables. There are also a pool and a restaurant. ⊗ *Contrada Gangivecchio, follow the signs from Gangi* • *Map E3* • *0921 602 147* • *No air con* • *www. gangivecchio.org* • *€€*

3 BB 22, Palermo

Each room in this centrally located B&B in a restored *palazzo* is unique. Expect feather tassels on the gilt bureau, hot pink terry-cloth-covered bath furniture and armoires with eastern motifs. Very nice staff, a bar and a charming terrace for breakfast. Free Internet.

⊗ *Palazzo Pantelleria, Largo Cavalieri di Malta 22* • *Map M3* • *091 326 214* • *www. bb22.it* • *€€€*

4 Sotto i Pini, Zafferana Etnea

This charming Art Nouveau villa is set in its own vineyards, olive groves and orchards, with views of Etna and the sea. Breakfast features organic, seasonal, local produce, much of it home-grown. ⊗ *Via A Diaz 208, Pisano* • *Map G3* • *095 956 69* • *www.sottoipini.it* • *€€*

5 Talia, Modica

Various small stone houses in Modica's ancient ghetto have been sensitively renovated and linked together via original terraced gardens and stone staircases. The rooms are minimally decorated with a mix of Sicilian materials and elements of high design. ⊗ *Via Exaudinos 1/9* • *Map G6* • *0932 752 075* • *www. casatalia.it* • *€€€*

6 Azienda Agricola Fattoria Mosè, Agrigento

Choose from self-catering apartments with private terrace or a B&B option on this working farm. The apartments are housed in converted stables, while the B&B is in the farmhouse itself. Minimum two-night stay. ⊗ *Via M Pascal 4, Villaggio Mosè* • *Map D4* • *0922 606 115 or 360 412 921* • *www. fattoriamose.com* • *€€€*

7 Locanda COS, Vittoria

Restored farmhouses on the grounds of the COS winery have been made into romantic apartments with high domed ceilings and balconies. Gorgeous pool area, winery tours on request and traditional food. ⊗ *SP3, Km 14,300* • *Map F5* • *0932 876 145* • *www.cosvittoria.it* • *€€€*

8 Casa Migliaca, Pettineo

A 17th-century estate with stone buildings, terraces and organic farm. Half board only. ⊗ *Contrada Migliaca, Pettineo (between Cefalù and Santo Stefano di Camastra)* • *Map E2* • *0921 336 722* • *www. casamigliaca.com* • *€€€*

9 La Zagara, Furci Siculo

In a quiet village near Taormina, just steps from the beach. The five rooms all have private bathroom and balcony with sea views. ⊗ *Via Manzoni 5* • *Map H3* • *338 217 89 89* • *www.lazagarabeb.it* • *€€*

10 Tenuta San Michele, Santa Venerina

Located on a winery estate on the eastern slope of Mount Etna. Rooms are spacious, and the grounds are beautiful, with a pool and ample views and the restaurant serves tasty, traditional food. ⊗ *Via Zafferana 13* • *Map G3* • *095 950 520* • *www.murgo.it* • *€€*

Agriturismo *means working farms and estates that open their homes or grounds to guests. See www.agriturist.it for details.*

Left **Bosco Falconeria Azienda Biologica** Right **Il Pescatore**

Self-Catering and Villas

1 Azienda Agrituristica Villa Levante, Castelbuono

Three nicely restored self-catering apartments are set in the towers of a 19th-century castle with stained glass, pretty gardens and a farm producing olive oil. Mountain-bike and hike on marked trails or walk in to Castel-buono. ✆ *Via Isnello • Map E3 • 0921 671 914 • www. villalevante.it • €€*

2 Bosco Falconeria Azienda Biologica, Partinico

These ecologically friendly apartments on a farm have terraces with views over the countryside and full kitchens in which to prepare meals with fresh produce bought from the farm itself. Within easy reach of Palermo and the beaches and monuments of western Sicily. ✆ *SS 113, Km 318 • Map C2 • 328 759 65 76 • No credit cards • No air conditioning • www. boscofalconeria.it • €*

3 Enza Marturano, Lipari

In the centre of Lipari, not far from the Marina Corta *(see p12)*. Four bright private rooms with cooking facilities are grouped around a communal sitting room, kitchen and terrace. The friendly owner can make recommendations for excursions. ✆ *Via Maurolico 35 • Map G1 • 368 322 49 97 • No credit cards • www. enzamarturano.it • €€*

4 Il Pescatore, Marinella di Selinunte

Il Pescatore is located in a family home in the fishing village of Marinella di Selinunte. Seven rooms share kitchen and laundry facilities and there are two terraces: one for dining, the other with a view of the temples. ✆ *Via Castore e Polluce 31 • Map B4 • 0924 46 303 • No credit cards • No air conditioning • €*

5 Apartments Giudecca, Cefalù

Apartments for rent to the east of Cefalù, at the small tourist port, with a view over the clear blue water and rock formations. The apartments are built on a cliffside, with shady balconies overlooking the sea, and steps down the cliffs. ✆ *Via Candeloro 127 • Map E2 • 0921 922 339 • www.bookingcefalu.com • €€€€€*

6 The Parker Company

This reputable company has four exclusive and luxurious properties in Sicily. They occasionally have representatives on site, and can help clients plan itineraries, secure hire cars and organize day trips. ✆ *From the UK: 0800 032 17 04; from North America: 1800 280 28 11; from elsewhere: 1781 596 82 82 • www. theparkercompany.com*

7 Cuendet

This Italian/Swiss company has been renting villas, mostly in Italy, since 1974. Choose from 172 quality properties. ✆ *0412 516 100 • www.cuendet.com*

8 Italian Villas

Another company with a great selection of properties, both in Sicily and on the island of Pantelleria. They provide assistance with car and mobile phone rentals, on- or off-site catering services and winery tours. ✆ *From the UK: 020 7101 9219; from North America: 1877 993 01 00; from elsewhere: 1514 393 88 44 • www. italianvillas.com*

9 Rentvillas.com

In operation since 1984, this agency rents a range of European properties, and they offer around 25 options in Sicily. They can assist with travel plans, too. ✆ *From North America: 1800 726 67 02; from elsewhere: 1805 880 12 28 • www.rentvillas.com*

10 Reùsia Holiday Houses

Carefully selected villas in the countryside, by the sea and in Ragusa town centre are on offer through this company. Reùsia also provides a range of other services from babysitting to guided tours and cookery classes. ✆ *348 604 25 08 • www.reusia.com*

Above **Hotel Victoria**

Price Categories

For a standard, double room per night (with breakfast if included), taxes and extra charges.

€	under €50
€€	€50–€100
€€€	€100–€150
€€€€	€150–€200
€€€€€	over €200

Pensione and Monasteries

1 Pocho, San Vito lo Capo

Nice small *pensione* with 12 comfortable rooms, some decorated with items from a traditional Sicilian puppet theatre. There is a great terrace restaurant *(see p97)*, fabulous sea views and a beach nearby. A swimming pool and cookery courses are also on offer. ◈ *Contrada Makari • Map B2 • 0923 972 525 • Dis. access • www. pocho.it • €€€*

2 Pensione Tranchina, Scopello

A 10-room *pensione* in this tiny fishing village. Rooms are nicely decorated with iron or wooden bedsteads, and several have a view of the sea. The ground-floor sitting area has a fireplace, and the owners cook excellent Sicilian cuisine, mostly fresh seafood and vegetables from their garden. ◈ *Via A Diaz 7 • Map C2 • 0924 541 099 • www.pensione tranchina.com • €€*

3 Hotel Victoria, Taormina

A comfortable *pensione* that counts Oscar Wilde among its former guests. The breakfast room has a terrace and view down onto the Corso. There are three parking spots. ◈ *Corso Umberto 81 • Map H3 • 0942 23 372 • www. albergovictoria.it • €€–€€€*

4 Hotel Miramare, Selinunte

The charming Miramare overlooks the Mediterranean sea, and affords a breathtaking view of the nearby Acropolis of Selinute. The hotel has its own private beach, piano bar and pizzeria restaurant. The owners and staff are welcoming and helpful. ◈ *Via Pigafetta 2 • Map B3 • 0924 46 666 • Dis. access • www.hotelmiramare selinute.it • €€*

5 Il Giardino del Barocco, Noto

This small *pensione* is set in a magnificent historic palace with a leafy courtyard garden, offering an oasis of calm in the city centre. ◈ *Via Aurispa Giovanni 77 • Map G5 • 0931 573 919 • www. ilgiardinodelbarocco.it • €€*

6 La Giara, Nicolosi

Spacious rooms and colourful decor make this an appealing base for exploring the area around Mount Etna. There is an ample terrace with views up to the volcano. ◈ *Via Pirandello 26 • Map G3 • 347 9025 04 93 • www. giara.it • €€*

7 Albergo Domus Mariae, Syracuse

The Ursuline sisters run a hotel in a restored 19th-century *palazzo* on Ortygia. All the 16 modern rooms have air conditioning; some have a sea view. Books up quickly.

◈ *Via Vittorio Veneto 76 • Map H5 • 0931 24 854 • www.domusmariae benessere.com • €€€€*

8 Monastero di San Benedetto, Modica

A few minutes' walk from the station, this monastery, founded in 1892, has single bedrooms and a refectory. It is mainly for religious retreats. ◈ *Via Santa Maria e Sant'Antonio 7 • Map G6 • 0932 941033 • No credit cards • No air conditioning • €*

9 Giardino sul Duomo, Ragusa Ibla

A lovingly preserved historic building set in equally fine gardens, with stunning views over Ragusa's cathedral dome and town centre to the hills and valleys beyond. The six large, light rooms are furnished in an elegantly modern style. ◈ *Via Capitano Bocchieri 24 • Map F5 • 0932 682 157 • Dis. access • www. giardinosulduomo.it • €€*

10 SoleLuna della Solidarietà, Palermo

Each room here has its own private, though not en-suite, bathroom. The owner donates 5 per cent of her proceeds to a local youth group; she also offers tours of Palermo. ◈ *Via Vincenzo Riolo 7 • Map L2 • 091 581 671 • Dis. access • No credit cards • www.solelunabed andbreakfast.org • €€*

Left **Kalura Hotel** Right **Hotel Signum**

🔟 Resort Hotels

1 Raya, Panarea
A study in relaxation, where whitewashed buildings with large terraces look out over the island to the sea. There is a restaurant right over the sea serving fresh fish dinners on a terrace lit with oil lamps. The staff can arrange excursions. Children under 12 years are not allowed. ◈ *Via San Pietro • Map G1 • 090 983 013 • Closed Nov–Mar • www.hotelraya.it • €€€€€*

2 Hotel Signum, Salina
A lovely location on a vine-covered hillside. Thirty rooms equipped with ceiling fans are set in a typical Aeolian house and outbuildings. White-washed walls surround terraces looking down to the sea. The restaurant is highly recommended. ◈ *Via Scalo 15, Malfa • Map G1 • 090 98 44 222 • Closed Jan–Mar • www.hotelsignum.it • €€€€€*

3 Capofaro Malvasia & Resort, Salina
Eighteen luxurious rooms with balconies open onto sea views at the Tasca d'Almerita family's five-star resort. The whitewashed buildings are set off by splashes of bougainvillea. Swimming pool, cooking classes, sea access, plus a restaurant serving island cuisine and all the wines from the Regaleali range. ◈ *Via Faro 3 • Map G1 • 090 984 4330/1 • www.capofaro.it • €€€€€*

4 Etna Golf Hotel & Resort, Castiglione di Sicilia
This resort on the slopes of Mount Etna has an 18-hole golf course, tennis courts, pool, gym and spa. Helicopter excursions and trekking can also be arranged, and small culinary fairs are often held on the grounds. Easy access to Taormina and Catania. ◈ *SS 120, Km 200 • Map G3 • 0942 986 384 • www.etnagolfresort.it • €€€*

5 Hotel Villa Sant' Andrea, Taormina
Rooms with terraces and sea views are housed in a restored 19th-century villa beneath Monte Tauro. There is dining under the palm trees and a private beach at Mazzarò. ◈ *Via Nazionale 137, Mazzarò • Map H3 • 0942 627 12 00 • Closed Nov–Mar • www.hotelvillasantandrea.com • €€€€€*

6 Kalura Hotel, Cefalù
This modern hotel has 72 rooms and a range of facilities, including a pool, private beach, billiards, tennis, mountain bikes and sailing. Horse riding can also be organized. ◈ *Via Vincenzo Cavallaro 13 • Map E2 • 0921 421 354 • www.hotel-kalura.com • €€€€€*

7 Atlantis Bay, Taormina Mare
A luxurious hotel with full-service spa and private beach. The pool and terrace for dining are literally on the water's edge. Elegant rooms have a private terrace with views of the bay; the enormous suites have fully stocked wine coolers. ◈ *Via Nazionale 161 • Map H3 • 0942 618 011 • www.atlantisbay.it • €€€€€*

8 La Dimora di Spartivento, Ragusa
In a rural setting with great views over the Hyblean plateau and Modica to the sea, this hotel has 16 large, comfortable rooms and a pool with a small waterfall. ◈ *SS 115, Km 323 • Map F5 • 0932 186 5377 • www.dimoradispartivento.it • €€*

9 Verdura Golf & Spa Resort, Sciacca
This top-class resort has its own stretch of coastline, three golf courses and a spa. Its location makes it ideal for trips to Agrigento and Selinunte. ◈ *SS 115, Km 131 • Map C4 • 0925 998 001 • Dis. access • www.verduraresort.com • €€€€€*

10 Approdo di Ulisse, Favignana
A tastefully designed resort of whitewashed bungalows and cottages by a series of tiny caves on the west side of the island. Pool, tennis and diving available. ◈ *C/da Calagrande • Map A3 • 0923 921 125 • www.aurumhotel.it • €€*

Streetsmart

Note: *Unless otherwise stated, all hotels accept credit cards, and have en-suite bathrooms and air conditioning.*

Price Categories

For a standard, double room per night (with breakfast if included), taxes and extra charges.

€ under €50
€€ €50–€100
€€€ €100–€150
€€€€ €150–€200
€€€€€ over €200

Above **Residence Guidaloca**

TOP 10 Campsites and Hostels

1 Agorà Hostel, Catania

Located near the Duomo, Roman ruins and colourful Pescheria market, this hostel has no curfew and offers accommodation in dormitories or private rooms. Its lively bar and restaurant is open to the public (see p69). ◎ Piazza Currò 6 • Map G4 • 095 723 30 10 • Dis. access • www.agorahostel.com • €

2 Ostello di Palermo Baia dei Coralli, Palermo

Just a few steps from the beach in a small seaside resort, this hostel sleeps 76 in double or four-bed rooms, each with a private bath. A short bus ride from Palermo town. ◎ Via Plauto 27, Sferracavallo • Map D2 • 091 679 78 07 • www.aighostels.it • €

3 Taormina's Odyssey, Taormina

There's a friendly atmosphere at this hostel in the residential part of Taormina, just a short walk from the centre. Dormitory or private rooms available. ◎ Via G Martino, Traversa A, 2 • Map H3 • 0942 24 533 • Dis. access • www.taorminaodyssey.com • €

4 Residence Guidaloca, Scopello

This residence provides small bungalows and apartments that can accommodate any size of group, each with kitchenette and terrace. The park-like setting includes terraces under olive trees. Near the beach. ◎ Guidaloca, Scopello • Map C2 • 0924 39 025 • www.residenceguidaloca.it • €€€

5 Miramare Camping Village, Favignana

Each of the attractive Mediterranean-style bungalows here has its own garden and veranda, and there is also an area for tents. The beach has a diving centre, beach volleyball and children's activities. A mini-market and bar complete the picture. ◎ Strada Provinciale Punta Sottile • Map B3 • 0923 921 330 • www.miramareresidence.it • €€€€

6 Camping Il Forte, Marzamemi

This camping village with bungalows and ample parking is near a sandy beach. Facilities include public telephones, restaurant, bar and market, as well as diving, boat, bike and scooter hire, and organized entertainment. ◎ Marzamemi • Map G6 • 0931 841 011 • Dis. access • www.ilfortevillage.it • €€

7 Camping Village Kamemi, Ribera

This campsite provides 170 tent and caravan spots, bungalows for rent, adult and children's pool, tennis, restaurant and beach access. ◎ C/da Cameni Superiore, Seccagrande, Ribera • Map C4 • 0925 69 212 • Dis. access • www.kamemivillage.com • €€

8 Camping Baia Unci, Lipari

On one of the most beautiful bays on the island of Lipari, this well-shaded campsite takes tents, campervans and caravans. There are also fully furnished, air-conditioned bungalows for 2–6 people. ◎ Via Marina Garibaldi, Canetto • Map G1 • 090 981 19 09 • www.campingbaiaunci.it • €

9 Camping La Focetta Sicula, Sant'Alessio Siculo

This campsite right by the sea also has 85 beds in fully furnished bungalows and mobile homes equipped with air conditioning, heating and with a shaded terrace or veranda. ◎ Contrada Siena 40 • Map H3 • 0942 751 657 • www.lafocetta.it • €

10 Camping Costa Ponente, Cefalù

A three-star campsite with spots for tents and caravans, swimming pool, tennis and access to the beach below. Facilities include a bar, self-service restaurant and a small market. ◎ Loc. Ogliatrillo, state road 113, Km 190 • Map E2 • 0921 420 085 • No credit cards • Closed Nov–Mar • €€

General Index

Index

Index

Acknowledgments

Main Contributor
Elaine Trigiani is a Sicilian-American art historian living in Italy since 1998. A certified olive-oil taster, she designs and leads travel programmes, as well as running cooking classes in Sicily, Tuscany and the USA.

Produced by Sargasso Media Ltd, London

Editorial Director Zoë Ross
Art Editor Janis Utton
Editor John Sinclair
Picture Research Helen Stallion
Proofreader Stewart J Wild
Indexer Hilary Bird
Editorial Assistance Louis Mendola

Main Photographers
Demetrio Carrasco & Nigel Hicks
Additional Photography
John Heseltine, Ian O'Leary, Conchita Vecchio

Illustrator chrisorr.com

For Dorling Kindersley
Publisher Douglas Amrine
Senior Designer Ian Midson
Revisions Designers
Rahul Kumar, Sonal Modha, Susana Smith
Senior Editor Lucinda Cooke
Senior Cartographic Editor Casper Morris
Revisions Team
Ashwin Adimari, Marta Bescos Sanchez, Imogen Corke, Michelle Crane, Rebecca Flynn, Fay Franklin, Rhiannon Furbear, Camilla Gersh, Claire Jones, Maite Lantaron, Hayley Maher, Alison McGill, Vikki Nousiainen, Rada Radojicic, Lucy Richards, Sands Publishing Solutions, Nikky Twyman
Factcheckers
Sarah Lane, Cathia Licitra, Pia Morabito, Maria Consuelo Petrolo, Conchita Vecchio
DTP Jason Little
Production Melanie Dowland
Maps John Plumer

Special Assistance
The author would like to thank the following people for their assistance: Corrado Assenza, Alessandro Barellini, Francesca Canizaro, Leonardo Canizaro, Mark Canizaro, Paul Canizaro, Robert Canizaro, Carmela Como, Frank Cornelissen, Jean and Jim Enochs, Joe Giattina, Giuseppe Grappolini, Leonie Loudon, Nino Norrito, Dell and Gianni Palazzolo, Kate Papacosmos, Mike Sacks, Giovanni Saladino, Mariella Sciacca, Adri Trigiani, David Perin Trigiani

Picture Credits
a-above; b-below/bottom; c-centre; f-far; l-left; r-right; t-top.

The publishers would like to thank the following individuals, companies and picture libraries for permission to reproduce their photographs:

4CORNERS: SIME / Paolo Giocoso 9cr.

Acknowledgments

AGF: Sintesi 131tl;
AGRITURISMO VULTAGGIO
97tl; ALAMY IMAGES:
CuboImages srl/Gimmi 54bl;
CuboImages srl/Michele Bella
89tl; Bob Turner 129tl;
ANTICA DOLCERIA
BONAJUTO: 74tl.

BOSCO FALCONERIA: 144tl.

CANALI PHOTOBANK: 43r,
60tl, 60b, 114tl; CARLO
PELLEGRINO & C. S.p.A.:
72bc, 72cra, 96tr; CENTRALE
PALACE HOTEL, Palermo:
142tr; CEPHAS: Alan Proust
58tr, 73r; Mick Rock 72tl, 72tr;
CLUB MED: 146tr; CORBIS: 1,
4–5, 16t, 16–17, 17t, 17c, 17b,
33b, 34–5, 36tl, 36tr, 36b,
37r, 43t, 44b, 60tr, 78–9,
84–5, 90tl, 102–103, 104tr,
120–21, 124tl, 124tr; Robert
Harding World Imagery /
Matthew Williams-Ellis 66clb;
David Lees 55bc.

IL DAGHERROTIPO: Carlo
Columba 56tr, 57t; Willi La
Farina 56tl; Andrea Getuli 24–5,
108c; Giovanni Rinaldi 25cr,
30–31, 42tl, 42b, 56b, 58b,
109t.GRACI: 73c; GRAZIA
NERI: Franco Barbagallo 21c,
21b, 53t, 58tl, 59, 105tr, 131tr.

HOTEL DEL CORSO: 142tl;
HOTEL KALURA: 146tl;

HOTEL SIGNUM: 146tr;
HOTEL VICTORIA: 145tl.

INDEX, Firenze: 13cr, 61t;
Alberti 111l; Baldi 92b.

KOBAL COLLECTION:
Cristaldifilm/Films Ariane 61r.

LA CAPINERA: 107tl;
LOCANDA COS: 143tl.

MARIA CONSUELO PETROLO
123tr

NHPA: 132tr.

RESIDENCE GUIDALOCA:
147tl; RISTORANTE LA GAZZA
LADRA: 75tr, 125tl;
RISTORANTE MAJORE: 76tr.

SANVITOCOUSCOUS.COM:
57r.; SICULAMENTE: 67bl.

TRATTORIA DEI TEMPLI: 115tl.

ANTONIO ZIMBONE: 16b,
104tl.

All other images are
© Dorling Kindersley.
For further information see:
www.dkimages.com

Phrase Book

In an Emergency

Help!	**Aiuto!**	eye-yoo-toh!
Stop!	**Fermo!**	fair-moh!
Call a doctor	**Chiama un medico**	kee-ah-mah oon meh-dee-koh
Call an ambulance	**Chiama un' ambulanza**	kee-ah-mah oon am-boo-lan-tsa
Call the police	**Chiama la polizia**	kee-ah-mah lah pol-ee-tsee-ah
Call the fire brigade	**Chiama i pompier**	kee-ah-mah ee pom-pee-air-ee

Communication Essentials

Yes/No	**Si/No**	see/noh
Please	**Per favore**	pair fah-vor-eh
Thank you	**Grazie**	grah-tsee-eh
Excuse me	**Mi scusi**	mee skoo-zee
Hello	**Buon giorno**	bwon jor-noh
Goodbye	**Arrivederci**	ah-ree-veh-dair-chee
Good evening	**Buona sera**	bwon-ah sair-ah
What?	**Cosa?**	koh-sah?
When?	**Quando?**	kwan-doh?
Why?	**Perchè?**	pair-keh?
Where?	**Dove?**	doh-veh?

Useful Phrases

How are you?	**Come sta?**	koh-meh stah?
Very well, thank you	**Molto bene, grazie**	moll-toh beh-neh grah-tsee-eh
Pleased to meet you	**Piacere di conoscerla**	pee-ah-chair-eh dee-coh-noh-shair-lah
That's fine	**Va bene**	va beh-neh
Where is/are ...?	**Dov'è/ Dove sono ...?**	dov-eh/doveh soh-noh?
How do I get to ...?	**Come faccio per arrivare a ...?**	koh-meh fah-choh pair arri-var-eh ah ...?
Do you speak English?	**Parla inglese?**	par-lah een-gleh-zeh?
I don't understand	**Non capisco**	non ka-pee-skoh
I'm sorry	**Mi dispiace**	mee dee-spee-ah-cheh

Shopping

How much does this cost?	**Quant'è, per favore?**	kwan-teh pair fah-vor-eh?
I would like ...	**Vorrei ...**	vor-ray ...
Do you have ...?	**Avete ...?**	ah-veh-teh ...?
Do you take credit cards?	**Accettate carte di credito?**	ah-chet-tah-teh kar-teh dee creh-dee-toh?
What time do you open /close?	**A che ora apre/ chiude?**	ah keh or-ah ah-preh/kee-oo-deh?
this one	**questo**	kweh-stoh
that one	**quello**	kwell-oh
expensive	**caro**	kar-oh
cheap	**a buon prezzo**	ah bwon pret-soh
size (clothes)	**la taglia**	lah tah-lee-ah
size (shoes)	**il numero**	eel noo-mair-oh
white	**bianco**	bee-ang-koh
black	**nero**	neh-roh
red	**rosso**	ross-oh
yellow	**giallo**	jal-loh
green	**verde**	vair-deh
blue	**blu**	bloo

Types of Shop

bakery	**il forno /il panificio**	eel forn-oh /eel pan-ee-fee-choh
bank	**la banca**	lah bang-kah
bookshop	**la libreria**	lah lee-breh-ree-ah
cake shop	**la pasticceria**	lah pas-tee-chair-ee-ah
chemist	**la farmacia**	lah far-mah-chee-ah
delicatessen	**la salumeria**	lah sah-loo-meh-ree-ah
department store	**il grande magazzino**	eel gran-deh mag-gad-zee-noh
grocery	**alimentari**	ah-lee-men-tah-ree
hairdresser	**il parrucchiere**	eel par-oo-kee-air-eh
ice-cream parlour	**la gelateria**	lah jel-lah-tair-ree-ah
market	**il mercato**	eel mair-kah-toh
newsstand	**l'edicola**	leh-dee-koh-lah
post office	**l'ufficio postale**	loo-fee-choh pos-tah-leh
supermarket	**il supermercato**	eel su-pair-mair-kah-toh
tobacconist	**il tabaccaio**	eel tah-bak-eye-oh
travel agency	**l'agenzia di viaggi**	lah-jen-tsee-ah dee vee-ad-jee

Sightseeing

art gallery	**la pinacoteca**	lah peena-koh-teh-kah
bus stop	**la fermata dell'autobus**	lah fair-mah-tah dell ow-toh-booss
church	**la chiesa**	lah kee-eh-zah
	la basilica	lah bah-seel-i-kah
closed for holidays	**chiuso per le ferie**	kee-oo-zoh pair leh fair-ee-eh
garden	**il giardino**	eel jar-dee-no
museum	**il museo**	eel moo-zeh-oh
railway station	**la stazione**	lah stah-tsee-oh-neh
tourist information	**l'ufficio di turismo**	loo-fee-choh dee too-ree-smoh

Staying in a Hotel

Do you have any vacant rooms?	**Avete camere libere?**	ah-veh-teh kah-mair-eh lee-bair-eh?
double room	**una camera doppia**	oona kah-mair-ah doh-pee-ah
with double bed	**con letto matrimoniale**	kon let-toh mah-tree-moh-nee-ah-leh
twin room	**una camera con due letti**	oona kah-mair-ah kon doo-eh let-tee
single room	**una camera singola**	oona kah-mair-ah sing-goh-lah

| room with a bath/shower | una camera con bagno, con doccia | oona kah-mair-ah kon ban-yoh, kon dot-chah |
| I have a reservation | Ho fatto una prenotazione. | oh faht-toh oona preh-noh-tah-tsee-oh-neh |

Eating Out

Have you got a table for ...?	Avete una tavola per ...?	ah-veh-teh oona tah-voh-lah pair ...?
I'd like to reserve a table	Vorrei riservare una tavola	vor-ray ree-sair-vah-reh oona tah-voh-lah
breakfast	la colazione	lah koh-lah-tsee-oh-neh
lunch	il pranzo	eel pran-tsoh
dinner	la cena	lah cheh-nah
the bill	il conto	eel kon-toh
waitress	cameriera	kah-mair-ee-air-ah
waiter	cameriere	kah-mair-ee-air-eh
fixed price menu	il menù a prezzo fisso	eel meh-noo ah pret-soh fee-soh
dish of the day	il piatto del giorno	eel pee-ah-toh dell jor-no
starter	antipasto	an-tee-pass-toh
first course	il primo	eel pree-moh
main course	il secondo	eel seh-kon-doh
vegetables	contorni	eel kon-tor-noh
dessert	il dolce	eel doll-cheh
cover charge	il coperto	eel koh-pair-toh
wine list	la lista dei vini	lah lee-stah day vee-nee
glass	il bicchiere	eel bee-kee-air-eh
bottle	la bottiglia	lah bot-teel-yah
knife	il coltello	eel kol-tell-oh
fork	la forchetta	lah for-ket-tah
spoon	il cucchiaio	eel koo-kee-eye-oh

Menu Decoder

l'acqua minerale gassata/ naturale	lah-kwah mee-nair-ah-leh gah-zah-tah/ nah-too-rah-leh	mineral water fizzy/still
l'agnello	lah-niell-oh	lamb
l'aglio	lal-ee-oh	garlic
al forno	al for-noh	baked
alla griglia	ah-lah greel-yah	grilled
la birra	lah beer-rah	beer
la bistecca	lah bee-stek-kah	steak
il burro	eel boor-oh	butter
il caffè	eel kah-feh	coffee
la carne	la kar-neh	meat
carne di maiale	kar-neh dee mah-yah-leh	pork
la cipolla	la chip-oh-lah	onion
i fagioli	ee fah-joh-lee	beans
il formaggio	eel for-mad-joh	cheese
il fritto misto	eel free-toh mees-toh	mixed fried dish
la frutta	la froot-tah	fruit
frutti di mare	froo-tee dee mah-reh	seafood
i funghi	ee foon-ghee	mushrooms
i gamberi	ee gam-bair-ee	prawns
il gelato	eel jel-lah-toh	ice cream
l'insalata	leen-sah-lah-tah	salad
il latte	eel laht-teh	milk
il manzo	eel man-tsoh	beef
l'olio	loh-lee-oh	oil
il pane	eel pah-neh	bread
le patate	leh pah-tah-teh	potatoes
le patatine fritte	leh pah-tah-teen-eh free-teh	chips
il pepe	eel peh-peh	pepper
il pesce	eel pesh-eh	fish
il pollo	eel poll-oh	chicken
il pomodoro	eel poh-moh-dor-oh	tomato
il prosciutto	eel pro-shoo-toh	ham
il riso	eel ree-zoh	rice
il sale	eel sah-leh	salt
la salsiccia	lah sal-see-chah	sausage
il succo d'arancia/ di limone	eel soo-koh dah-ran-chah/ dee lee-moh-neh	orange/lemon juice
il tè	eel teh	tea
la torta	lah tor-tah	cake/tart
l'uovo	loo-oh-voh	egg
vino bianco	vee-noh bee-ang-koh	white wine
vino rosso	vee-noh ross-oh	red wine
le vongole	leh von-goh-leh	clams
lo zucchero	loh zoo-kair-oh	sugar
la zuppa	lah tsoo-pah	soup

Numbers

1	uno	oo-noh
2	due	doo-eh
3	tre	treh
4	quattro	kwat-roh
5	cinque	ching-kweh
6	sei	say-ee
7	sette	set-teh
8	otto	ot-toh
9	nove	noh-veh
10	dieci	dee-eh-chee
11	undici	oon-dee-chee
12	dodici	doh-dee-chee
13	tredici	tray-dee-chee
14	quattordici	kwat-tor-dee-chee
15	quindici	kwin-dee-chee
16	sedici	say-dee-chee
17	diciassette	dee-chah-set-teh
18	diciotto	dee-chot-toh
19	diciannove	dee-chah-noh-veh
20	venti	ven-tee
30	trenta	tren-tah
40	quaranta	kwah-ran-tah
50	cinquanta	ching-kwan-tah
60	sessanta	sess-an-tah
70	settanta	set-tan-tah
80	ottanta	ot-tan-tah
90	novanta	noh-van-tah
100	cento	chen-toh
1,000	mille	mee-leh
2,000	duemila	doo-eh mee-lah
1,000,000	un milione	oon meel-yoh-neh

Time

one minute	un minuto	oon mee-noo-toh
one hour	un'ora	oon or-ah
a day	un giorno	oon jor-noh
Monday	lunedì	loo-neh-dee
Tuesday	martedì	mar-teh-dee
Wednesday	mercoledì	mair-koh-leh-dee
Thursday	giovedì	joh-veh-dee
Friday	venerdì	ven-air-dee
Saturday	sabato	sah-bah-toh
Sunday	domenica	doh-meh-nee-kah